THE
BARTENDER'S
BOOK

This edition published by Parragon in 2010

Parragon
Queen Street House
4 Queen Street
Bath BA1 1HE
UK

ISBN: 978-1-4075-3396-4

Printed in China

Created and produced by Butler & Tanner Printers Ltd
Cover design by Parragon

Additional text by Lisa Hughes and Sarah Johnstone

Contributing photographers: Mike Cooper, Charlie Richards, Günter Beer and Carole McDonald. Special thanks to Beau Field and Raymond Law at Mu Mu's in Bristol, to Bibas in Bristol and to Passvale Farm in Somerset for their help with location photography.

Additional photography: endpapers ©istockphoto.com/leadinglights; page 6 ©istockphoto.com/erichood; page 14 bottom right ©istockphoto.com/itographer; page 15 ©istockphoto.com/nickfree; page 17 bottom ©istockphoto.com/dny59; page 18 top ©istockphoto.com/beans-; page 18 bottom ©istockphoto.com/ivanmateev; page 22 top middle ©istockphoto.com/sasodo; page 23 top right ©istockphoto.com/dias46; page 25 ©istockphoto.com/2044photo; page 26 ©istockphoto.com/zonecreative; page 36 ©istockphoto.com/raatzie; page 42 ©istockphoto.com/luisportugal; page 46 ©istockphoto.com/muratkoc; page 52 ©istockphoto.com/chronistin; page 66 ©istockphoto.com/abzee; page 78 ©istockphoto.com/thedman; page 80 ©istockphoto.com/horst72; page 84 ©istockphoto.com/plainview.

Index by Nick Fawcett

WARNING
Recipes containing raw eggs are not suitable for the elderly, pregnant women or anyone recovering from an illness.

Please drink alcohol responsibly.

THE
BARTENDER'S
BOOK

Bath · New York · Singapore · Hong Kong · Cologne · Delhi · Melbourne

CONTENTS

FOREWORD
by ANGUS WINCHESTER

After nearly 70 years in the doldrums the cocktail, and those that preside over its making and creation, is staging a resurgence. But as with all things in the 21st century it has become a more complicated affair. The humble but proud bartender has been replaced by the ingredient and technique savvy mixologist or even the bar chef. The few bottles and juices of the classic bar have been buried under a welcome avalanche of weird and wonderful liquors, fruits and flavours from around the world. And no longer can the bartender, or amateur 'shaker-upper', look merely to the USA for guidance and inspiration – the rest of the world has caught up quickly with fine drinks and bars aplenty.

But many of the basics from yesteryear still apply. A great cocktail is still a balanced potion of strong and weak, sweet and sour ingredients perfectly chilled and served in good glassware. A great bar, regardless of location, still combines excellence of service and ambiance, product and passion. And it is still possible to replicate the experience in one's own home, as long as one remembers that one cannot make a good product without good ingredients, a decent knowledge of technique and a fine set of recipes to follow.

New drinks are created constantly, often with at least one eye on the classics that have gone before but with the other eye looking eagerly at the new liquids on offer. Some may be included in future books as fine as this one, others may only please those that were there at its birth, the recipe being only foggily remembered the next day. But the art of drinks making and the pleasure associated with it for all concerned will still be considered the most convivial of the culinary skills. And those that practise it, be they world renowned bar chefs or the home enthusiast, display a thirst for knowledge, a wonder at the array of flavours they have and no small degree of obsessive compulsive behaviour in their quest for excellence… and I for one am very grateful for those traits.

Cheers… may the best of your past be the worst of your future.

Angus Winchester is a roving drinks expert, dispensing fine cocktails and sage advice to drinkers and those that serve them around the world. He lives at 38,000 feet, has worked in several of the world's top bars and has drunk in all of them.

THE BARTENDER'S BOOK
INTRODUCTION

We've come a long way since the days when a cocktail meant a rather sickly, garish liquid, often ready-mixed, with a paper umbrella balanced on the rim of the glass. Of course, if sweetshop colours and kitsch are what you like, each to their own and there's nothing wrong with that, but elegance, sophistication and indeed glamour is the modern fashion in cocktails.

This means that in the world of cocktails there is a renewed focus on fresh, high-quality ingredients and sometimes subtle, sometimes startling, flavour combinations. Whether in a bar or at home, skilfully mixed drinks, carefully balanced to the specific taste of the person who's about to drink them is the order of the day.

BECOME A GREAT BARTENDER

To be a great bartender you must combine the precision of a scientist with the creativity of an artist. A great bartender is both a technician and a chef; organised, efficient and with a thorough understanding of the tools of the trade. Yet sensitive, experimental and with a flair for the theatrical. To be a great bartender you must be equally at home in the laboratory of your bar workspace and on stage, attending to your guests' every need and presenting your creations with a dramatic flourish.

Don't be put off, however. Becoming a great bartender is certainly an achievable aspiration, especially with this volume tucked beside your ice bucket. But remember that substance and style are both vital for great bartending.

To this end, *The Bartender's Book* inducts the reader into the mysteries of mixology; the science of – and the secret to – the finest cocktails. In this section aspiring bartenders can learn how to shake, stir, strain and blend. There are instructions for constructing the perfect ice cube, and the complexities of layering, floating and muddling are all made crystal clear.

The book also contains a range of other resources, including information on how to stock your own bar, a list of the tools of the bartender's trade and a glossary of glasses. This explains how each glass got its name and when it should be used, as well as why it is important to use the right glass for a particular drink.

THE SOURCES
OF SUCCESS

A good bartender has a real feel for the essential elements of a good cocktail, which is why *The Bartender's Book* features a comprehensive lexicon of over 300 different drinks. From familiar spirits, wines and beers through to more unusual liqueurs, flavourings and soft drinks. This section of the book groups ingredients derived from the same raw materials together and explains how they're made, how they're used and how they're served.

It also offers some interesting insights into the history of many of the ingredients. These handy nuggets of often quirky information have been designed to catch the attention and they will help bartenders keep the conversational flow going while guests are waiting for their drinks to be mixed and poured.

A COMPENDIUM
OF COCKTAILS

At the heart of this book are over 400 cocktail recipes. These are grouped by the time of day or occasion on which you might enjoy them and each group is headed with a statement cocktail, which epitomises that particular moment.

From the traditional but mighty Martini to the new classic, the Cosmopolitan, via the Margarita, Daiquiri and Caipirinha, all the famous names are here, but there is also a wide range of lesser known recipes that are due for a revival, as well as up-to-date and slightly unusual concoctions, featuring more obscure spirits and fresh fruit and herbs. The selection is broad and deep, and somewhere on this glorious spectrum you'll undoubtedly find a cocktail to fit any event or mood.

Each recipe has details of how many it serves and is accompanied by an icon, which corresponds to the pictures in the glasses section and indicates which glass or glasses should be used for each cocktail. Many of the recipes also feature additional information or details of the story behind a particular cocktail.

This section also includes recipes for a choice selection of delicious and refreshing non-alcoholic cocktails, often known by the jaunty soubriquet 'mocktails'. So no one need feel left out – whether they're the designated driver, haven't yet reached the legal drinking age or simply don't fancy an alcoholic tipple.

BEST BAR NONE

And finally, to complement this wealth of practical and stimulating information, throughout the recipe section there are also features on some of the best bars in the world. There are ten in total, one from each of the world's top cities for drinking, each of which has its own unique and sometimes offbeat attractions. From cosy snugs to cosmopolitan hangouts, from vertigo-inducing venues to sand-between-the-toes

beach bars, these are places to visit if you should be lucky enough to have the opportunity. However, if, on the other hand, you won't be travelling further than the local off-licence this week, you can still soak up their ambience and let their ethos inspire you.

Equally useful behind the counter of a neighbourhood bar or on your coffee table at home, *The Bartender's Book* is informative, educational, entertaining and – like a great cocktail – a sheer delight. It's a one-stop shop for every aspiring bartender and adventurous drinker, so sit back, absorb and enjoy. Then get up and start shaking and stirring.

On a more sombre and serious note, the purpose of this book is to encourage the enjoyment of fine cocktails and other drinks. This volume is not intended to promote the over-consumption of alcohol. When treated responsibly, alcohol is, of course, a pleasing mood-enhancer, but inappropriate imbibing can lead to social and health problems, for individuals and indeed society at large. As a consequence, the publishers of *The Bartender's Book* would like to counsel readers to consume cocktails and any other alcoholic drink wisely, so don't over do it.

HOW TO USE THE RECIPES

At the heart of this bartender's guide are over 400 cocktail recipes. The recipes, which start on page 88, have been researched and collated from a wide range of sources. As a result, you'll find that most use measures, but a few use metric and/ or imperial measurements.

Unfortunately there are no international standards for bar measurements. In Europe a cocktail measure is usually 25 ml or approximately ¾ fl oz, which is where a jigger makes life a lot easier, although an accurate measuring jug is very useful too.

With the measures given in these recipes, though, bear in mind that it is essentially about the ratio of the base spirit to the modifier, the juice, champagne or cream that holds the drink together and actually turns it into a cocktail.

As with any recipe, to get the required result you need to follow the instructions carefully. If the recipe says chill the glass, chill it. If it tells you to fill the glass with ice, fill it. If it asks for cracked ice, don't use crushed ice. It's all in the detail, so don't be sloppy.

However, having said that, a good bartender will always fine-tune a cocktail and once you've mastered the basic recipe, try substituting one ingredient for another similar one, adjusting the quantities slightly or seeing what effect a different garnish has. If you taste the resulting cocktails side by side it will help you develop your own palate and ultimately mix better drinks.

Where the recipe calls for ice other than ordinary ice cubes, then this is specified in the list of ingredients.

GARNISHES

From the classic cocktail cherry or olive to citrus slices, mini fruit kebabs, edible flowers and kitschy accessories if you must, garnishes are part of the cocktail experience and decorating a cocktail is part of the fun. However, garnishes can also contribute to the taste of a cocktail, particularly when it comes to lemon, orange, lime and even grapefruit peel.

For a twist of peel, use a special citrus stripper, vegetable peeler or small sharp knife. Try to keep the pith to a minimum and cut a piece of skin length-wise. Twist this just above the surface of the drink, rind-side down, to release the citrus oil, and either hang it on the glass or drop it in. For a spiral, start at the top of the fruit and work your way around it.

KEY TO SYMBOLS

☆ 'Classic' cocktail

🍸 Cocktail or martini glass

🍸 Highball glass

🥃 Lowball glass

🥂 Champagne flute

🍷 Wine glass

🥃 Shot glass

🥃 Brandy snifter

🍸 Sour glass

🥤 Hurricane glass

🍸 Coupette glass

🥂 Pousse-café glass

☕ Irish coffee glass

🍺 Mug or tankard

🍍 Fresh pineapple

TOOLS
OF THE TRADE

What equipment you need in your bar or at home depends very much on whether you're the type of person who's determined to have all the latest gadgets and gismos, or whether you're prepared to make do with what you've got. Either way, keep your bar area clean and tidy and your professionalism will undoubtedly impress your guests.

JIGGER

If you're making mixed cocktails, a jigger is essential, because it's the bartender's basic measuring tool. There are different styles, but the most common and useful type is made from metal and double-ended, with one cup holding 25 ml/2.5 cl/ approximately ¾ fl oz or one measure, and the other holding 50 ml/5 cl/ 1¾ fl oz or two measures. The cups may also be marked with lines every 10 ml/10 cl/⅓ fl oz.

Optics aren't too expensive and they can make it easier to organise your space, but they are not essential.

SHAKER

The other essential for mixed cocktails is a shaker. Many professional bartenders prefer a Boston shaker, which consists of two cups, one of which can be used for measuring and stirring, which fit together tightly. The drawback to the Boston shaker, though, is that you need a separate strainer, such as a hawthorn strainer, which you hold over the top of the shaker as you pour.

Consequently, you may prefer to get a standard cocktail shaker, which also consists of two sections that fit together snugly, but which has a built-in strainer as well.

BAR SPOON

Of course, you can make do with a spoon from the kitchen, but a proper bar spoon has a small bowl and a long handle that allows you to muddle, mix and stir with ease. You will have to raid the cutlery drawer for a teaspoon and a tablespoon, though, as you'll need these for measuring.

MUDDLER

For advanced mixing, particularly if you're mashing up citrus fruit or crushing herbs, you need a muddler. This is a chunky wooden tool with a straight shaft and a rounded end, which can also be employed to make cracked ice. However, if you haven't got a muddler you can also do the job with a mortar and pestle or a good old wooden spoon.

MIXING GLASS

Any vessel that holds about half a litre/1 pint of liquid can be used for mixing drinks in, especially if you're making several servings at once. A jug with a spout, to prevent the ice from slipping into the glass, is good, but not vital.

BLENDER

You'll find a jug blender very useful for making a wide range of cocktails, particularly fruit- and cream-based ones, especially if it's got two speeds, so you can blend gently or vigorously. However, it is a good idea to get a fairly powerful one that is also able to chop and crush ice in bulk, although manual ice crushers are available.

JUICER

A traditional ridged half-lemon shape on a saucer will work perfectly well if you only require relatively small amounts of juice. There is also a gadget called a citrus spout, which screws into a lemon or lime and is useful for obtaining tiny quantities.

BOTTLE OPENER

A bottle opener is a simple, but efficient tool and you'll almost certainly have one of these already, although if you want to invest in a heavy-duty professional model that attaches to the wall or a counter top you'll be able to open bottles at top speed.

CORKSCREW

Again, there are many styles of corkscrew available, but whether it's a classic corkscrew with a metal spiral attached to a handle or a complex high-tech device that utilises the principles of physics to the full, choose one that you know you can operate quickly and easily.

STOPPERS AND POURERS

A wine bottle stopper – the vacuum ones are good – and a champagne bottle stopper, which will keep the fizz in, are worth having. If you use a lot of cordials, you might like to buy a set of pourers, which fit into the top of the bottle and allow you to splash liquids into glasses with a certain panache.

13

CHOPPING BOARD AND KNIFE

You'll need a small chopping board and a sharp knife for preparing fruit and garnishes. To pare off orange or lemon peel a specialist piece of equipment called a citrus stripper is handy, but a potato peeler will do the same job, although with slightly less finesse.

ICE BUCKET

You can press pretty much any decent-sized container into service as an ice bucket, but it's handy if it has a lid to slow down the melting process. Use tongs to pick up the cubes.

Of course, a ready supply of ice is vital for making cocktails and if your bar is located some distance away from the freezer you might consider investing in a small, portable ice-maker. However, ice is cheap to buy in bulk and a mini fridge to keep some of your cocktail constituents cold might be a more sensible and economical purchase.

SWIZZLE STICKS

If style and sophistication is the effect you're endeavouring to create, paper parasols won't provide it, but if you're after a kitschy retro feel then swizzle sticks are the answer, particularly if you search out vintage ones, plus they can be used for gentle stirring and to stab wayward garnishes.

GLASSES

The bare minimum is wine glasses and tumblers, but there are many different types of cocktail glass, and many corresponding reasons for serving specific cocktails in them (see pages 16-19), so most bartenders will probably want to start their own collection.

THE BASIC INGREDIENTS

When you're stocking your bar you'll obviously need the ingredients for any specific cocktails you intend to make, and you'll want to buy any spirits that are particular favourites, but there are a number of items that any good bartender really should have to hand.

SPIRITS AND WINES

Gin
Vodka
Brandy
Rum
Tequila
Blended whisky or whiskey
Dry vermouth
Sweet vermouth
Red wine
White wine
Champagne or sparkling wine
Beer and/or lager

LIQUEURS

Triple sec, curaçao, Cointreau
  or Grand Marnier
Blue curaçao
Kahlúa or other coffee liqueur
Pernod

MIXERS

Fruit juices (ideally freshly
  squeezed) and exotic juices
Sparkling mineral water
Soda water
Tonic water
Cola
Ginger ale

FLAVOURINGS AND GARNISHES

Angostura bitters
Worcestershire sauce
Tabasco sauce
Grenadine
Caster and icing sugar
Sugar syrup (see recipe, right,
  to make your own)
Fruit syrups (according
  to preference)
Salt

Maraschino cherries
Cocktail olives
Cocktail onions
Lemons, limes and oranges

SUGAR SYRUP

1 measure water
2 measures sugar

Bring the water to the boil in a saucepan. Remove from the heat and add the sugar, stirring until it's completely dissolved. Allow to cool, pour into a glass jar, seal and refrigerate. The syrup will keep for up to one month in the fridge. Quantities can be scaled up or down according to need.

THE BARTENDER'S GUIDE TO
GLASSES

Some people would say that if you serve a cocktail in the wrong glass it's hardly worth bothering, so this guide will ensure you get it right.

COCKTAIL OR MARTINI GLASS

COUPETTE GLASS

CLASSIC GLASSWARE

A traditional cocktail glass is sometimes referred to as a martini glass, champagne glass or stem cocktail glass. As with other stemware, the stem allows the drinker to hold the glass without affecting the temperature of the drink. The shape of the glass also helps keep the ingredients from separating while the stem keeps the drink cool. Cocktail glasses are usually used to serve cocktails without ice. They vary in size and volume, but normally hold between 85 ml/3 fl oz and 170 ml/6 fl oz. One variation of this glass is the double martini glass, which is taller and wider at the opening.

The most obviously recognisable cocktail glass, the conical martini glass, emerged with the Art Deco movement. It debuted at the 1925 Paris Exposition of Decorative Arts as a clever twist on the goblet. And like most stemmed glasses – or 'stemware' – this Y-shaped variety proved perfect for chilled cocktails, keeping people's hands from inadvertently warming their drinks. It gained popularity in Europe, particularly for Martinis, before proceeding to world domination after the Second World War.

Today's Coupette glass is based on the earlier champagne coupe, the saucer-shaped stem glass originally used for serving bubbly. Legend has it the coupe was modelled on a woman's breast. However, it was designed in 1663 so the story that it involved the anatomy of French queen Marie Antoinette must be apocryphal. To facilitate the rimming with salt necessary for Margaritas, the bowl of the coupette was widened. It's also used for Daiquiris.

CHAMPAGNE FLUTE

HIGHBALL GLASS

LOWBALL GLASS

The tall, thin flute glass has a hazy history. It dates back centuries, with its tapered design reducing the liquid's surface area and keeping champagne bubbly longer. However, it only became fashionable from the 1950s, possibly after Austrian glassmaker Claus Josef Riedel began researching the way different glass shapes affect taste. Since then, flutes have largely supplanted the coupe for champagne and champagne cocktails – helped by the fact that more flutes fit on a serving tray.

Highball glasses are tall tumblers suitable for simple drinks with a high proportion of mixer to spirit. They're not only an essential component of any home bar, but the title 'highball drinks' also encompasses a host of classic tipples, such as bourbon and water, scotch and soda, Bloody Marys and Vodka Tonics. Highball glasses are versatile enough to substitute for the similarly shaped, but slightly larger, Collins glass. They're related to larger Zombie and smaller Delmonico glasses too.

The terms 'lowball', 'rocks' and 'old-fashioned' are bandied around quite freely when referring to short, squat tumblers. As the second name suggests, they're perfect for holding ice and any spirit 'on the rocks' should be served in one of these. Lowball glasses are also popular for short mixed drinks, such as Old-fashioneds. Variants include the Sazerac glass, named after the cognac-and-bitters New Orleans cocktail. The double rocks glass, nicknamed 'the bucket', is used for tropical punch-style drinks.

SHOT GLASS

BRANDY SNIFTER

SOUR GLASS

This is the home-bar essential that most frequently moonlights as a novelty collector's item. The regular, unadorned shot glass holds just enough liquid to be downed in a mouthful and boasts a thick base to withstand being slammed on the bar after the neat spirits or mixed-spirits 'shooter' within has been consumed. Standard shot glasses are not just handy for toasts, they can stand in for jiggers too. And, decorated with a variety of designs, they've become popular souvenirs.

The brandy snifter stands apart from other stemware. Whereas most stemmed glasses keep warm human hands off chilled drinks, the short-stemmed, bowl-shaped snifter invites you to cradle it in your palm, warming its amber spirit. Its wide bottom creates a large surface area from which the brandy can evaporate, but the aroma is trapped as the glass narrows to a constricted mouth, allowing you to inhale it pleasurably before sipping. For best enjoyment, a snifter should only be one-third filled.

As one of the oldest family of mixed drinks, dating back to Jerry Thomas's seminal recipe book *How to Mix Drinks* (1862), sours, unsurprisingly, have been served up in all manner of glasses, from lowball to martini. However, sticklers for style will be pleased to learn that standard drinkware exists. The glass specified for whiskey sours, pisco sours and other citrus, sugar and spirits drinks is a smaller, modified champagne flute – narrow at the stem and widening out at the lip.

HURRICANE GLASS

POUSSE-CAFÉ GLASS

WINE GLASS

IRISH COFFEE GLASS

Most glasses are designed for and named after certain drinks, but this isn't exclusively true of the large (26 fl oz) hurricane glass. Although it was originally badged to contain the passionfruit-and-rum 'Hurricane' cocktail at New Orleans bar Pat O'Brien's, its pear shape is a homage to the hurricane lamp. Today it's associated with frozen and blended cocktails. A frozen Piña Colada is virtually unthinkable without this, and it's often used for flamboyantly named cocktails of the Sex-on-the-Beach ilk.

These small, narrow-stemmed vessels have a modified hourglass figure, making it easier to create layered drinks in them. Essentially, they're cordial glasses, with a flare at the top. Naturally, the art of any layered, rainbow drink is pouring the heaviest liqueur or syrup first and progressively layering lighter spirits. However, the bulb shape at this glass's bottom helps trap the lower layers and it's easy to drizzle liquids down the sides, thus causing less disturbance to those below.

White wine glasses tend to be smaller than red wine glasses, so use your judgement as to which will accommodate the particular cocktail you're making best. If a recipe mentions a goblet, however, go for a red wine glass or even a rounder balloon wine glass.

MUG

While not the height of sophistication, a mug is heatproof and is sometimes just what you need for a hot cocktail, especially if it's winter, the event is an outdoor one and guests may be wearing gloves.

The key feature of an Irish coffee glass is that it's made of heatproof glass, which makes it suitable for hot cocktails such as toddies. It's usually short-stemmed, with a handle, or may have a metal base and handle.

TANKARD

Occasionally recipes call for a tankard – traditionally a large, robust, one-handled drinking vessel, commonly made of silver, pewter or glass – but if you don't have one then a pint beer glass is a suitable substitute.

THE ART OF
MIXOLOGY

The secret of successful mixology lies in well-chosen spirits, freshly squeezed juices, just-crushed herbs and – crucially – the skilful deployment of the tricks and techniques of the bartender's trade.

As with cooking and architecture, when it comes to mixing drinks, sometimes less really is more and, although expert bartenders always like to experiment with new and unusual ingredients, nothing beats a well-made classic. There are about half a dozen basic methods for combining cocktail ingredients, and it helps to know the pros and cons, as well as the best way of performing each.

BUILDING, LAYERING AND FLOATING

Building a cocktail is the technical term for the simple task of pouring all the ingredients, one by one, over ice, into the glass in which the cocktail will be served. You might then stir them briefly.

Another important skill that the bartender must acquire is in the art of layering, which requires greater concentration, precision and a steadier hand. To make layered shooters or pousse-café drinks, you generally pour the heaviest liquid first, working through to the lightest. However, the real trick is the technique.

Either touch the top of the drink with a long-handled bar spoon and pour the liquid slowly over the back of it to disperse it across the top of the ingredients already in the glass, or pour the liquid down the twisted stem that many professional bar spoons have. Hold the spoon's flat disc just above the drink. A little practice helps perfect both these relatively challenging methods. Floating is usually the term used to describe adding the top layer.

SHAKING

This is the most flamboyant method of making a cocktail – the one that James Bond prefers for his Martinis and which added a bit of rocket fuel to Tom Cruise's career. Apart from so-called 'flair bartending' – otherwise known as showing off – shaking is good for chilling drinks and diluting them to just the right degree.

First, the shaker should be filled to the three-quarter level with ice cubes. (Never use crushed ice as it melts and makes the drink watery.) The ingredients are then poured over the ice and shaken briskly for about 10 seconds, with the shaker gripped firmly in both hands.

The cocktail is sufficiently chilled and ready to pour when condensation appears on the exterior of the shaker.

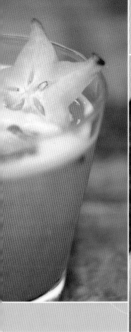

Strain the drink into a glass, leaving the ice behind in the shaker.

While it allows greater contact between cocktail and ice, and thus produces a colder drink than mere stirring, shaking also results in cloudier cocktails. It breaks tiny shards off the ice cubes, which then float in the liquid. The method also produces numerous tiny bubbles, which are great for drinks such as Margaritas.

However, opinion over Martinis remains divided. Some connoisseurs claim that shaking the gin can 'bruise' it and make it taste more bitter. Others counter that shaking dissolves the vermouth better, leaving it less oily. Even formal scientific studies comparing shaken and stirred Martinis have failed to settle the debate, so it remains a matter of personal preference.

STIRRING

Stirring is the purist's choice, the mixology method that aims to retain the strength of the spirit. By carefully using a glass or metal rod (swizzle stick), or even a long-handled bar spoon, you can avoid chipping the ice cubes and making the cocktail watery. Crushed ice is an absolute no-no here. Drinks should be gently stirred in a mixing glass or the bottom half of a Boston shaker. As soon as condensation appears on the outside of the glass or shaker, the drink should be strained into a glass. Because the goal is a strong drink, some expert bartenders argue that those cocktails containing just spirits and liqueurs – in other words no fruit juices – should always be stirred.

CHILL THE 'BURN'

Ice doesn't only chill cocktails; it mellows the 'burn' effect of strong spirits and enhances their flavours, so always follow recipe recommendations precisely.

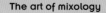

A TOUCH OF SPARKLE

To salt the rim of a glass, moisten the edge with a wedge of lime before turning the glass over and dipping it into a saucer of salt.

MUDDLING

In mixology, muddling isn't about confusion. Increasingly popular in bartending circles, it means to mash fruit or herbs to release their flavours and it's done with a wooden pestle-like implement called a muddler. The end used to crush ingredients is thicker and rounded; the opposite end, which is skinnier, is employed in stirring. Some also compare muddlers to rolling pins. The technique is to press down with a twisting action. Sometimes, a small amount of liquid will be added to facilitate muddling, but the majority of it is usually poured in later. Common muddled drinks include Caipirinhas (limes and sugar), Mojitos (mint leaves, sugar and soda) and Old-fashioneds (bitters and sugar syrup).

BLENDING

Electric blenders will mix ingredients that otherwise do not easily combine, so they are frequently employed when mixing alcohol with both fruit and fruit juice or alcohol with creamy ingredients. Strawberry Daiquiris and Piña Coladas are popular blended cocktails. As all the usual rules on ice are reversed in the blender and you do use crushed ice, it's also used for so-called frozen cocktail versions, such as Frozen Margaritas. The cocktail should be blended until it's smooth, but be careful not to overdo it. The crushed ice should also be added sparingly.

ICE

Good ice makes for good cocktails, so use filtered or still mineral water with a low mineral content. Ordinary tap water contains all sorts of additives and, while they are harmless, they do impart a flavour and will taint your ice.

If you want to make a very cold drink, fill the glass with ice, using large, solid lumps rather than small, fiddly ones. However, bear in mind that as the ice melts it will start to dilute your drink, so drink up relatively quickly or the taste will be impaired.

If a recipe calls for cracked ice you can buy this by the bag or make it yourself, by filling a plastic bag with cubes, covering it with a towel and then hitting it gently with a rolling pin. If you want crushed ice then either buy it from an off-licence or specialist ice supplier – or bag the ice as before and hit it harder.

Ordinary ice cubes are cloudy. This haziness is partly due to the additives, but it's also caused by tiny fractures, formed when the water freezes. If you want to make clear cubes – and it's a classy touch – use filtered or still mineral water. Boil it, to release any dissolved gases, cool it and pour it into an ice cube tray. As soon as the top of the cube has formed, puncture it. This will give the water inside a space to expand into, so it won't haze.

Once you've gone to the trouble of making good ice, don't ruin it by running the top of the tray under the tap to release it. Either flex the tray carefully or run water on to the underside of the tray. Never handle ice. Always use tongs, so you don't transfer residues from your fingers.

BEST RESULTS
For the best results, always chill your glasses beforehand by storing them in the fridge or placing them in the freezer for up to an hour.

THE BARTENDER'S
LEXICON
❖ OF COCKTAIL INGREDIENTS AND DRINKS ❖

Good bartenders are expected to be both gurus and geniuses. When it comes to what goes into a cocktail, they need to be the source of all knowledge, and, like an alchemist, they need to be able to turn those base elements into gold. To achieve this, good bartenders must have an intimate insight into the extensive range of cocktail ingredients, understanding the flavours and strengths of each one, what happens when they combine and what will work in place of a particular element, should it not be available.

The entries in this inventory are grouped by their major constituent or flavouring, so you'll find drinks distilled from grain, derived from sugar or flavoured with citrus fruits together. Being able to offer an interesting titbit or surprising fact as you serve a drink is also part of the bartender's act and if you spend some time browsing this inventory that's exactly the kind of information you'll pick up. However, if there's something specific you want to find, use the index.

DRINKS DISTILLED FROM GRAIN

SCOTCH WHISKY

There are over a hundred active distilleries in Scotland, located in six whisky-producing regions. Whisky has been made in Scotland since at least the 15th century, although its origins almost certainly go back several hundred years prior to that.

Scotch whisky is fermented grain that is distilled and then aged. The basic ingredients are spring water, malted barley and yeast, but the unique variations in taste come from the precise attributes of the local water and other ingredients, the configuration of the stills at the distillery, the type of barrels it's aged in and so on. For example, once barley has germinated, peat fires are sometimes used to dry it and this can impart a smoky peatiness to the flavour of the malted barley. This will then be present in the taste of the whisky that's made from it.

There are basically two kinds of Scotch whisky – malt and grain. Malt whisky is only made from malted barley and is distilled in a pot still. Grain whisky is made from malted and unmalted barley, as well as other grains, usually wheat, and is distilled in a continuous still. Malt whisky from a single distiller is bottled in small volumes as a single malt or combined with grain spirit to create blended whisky. Scottish grain whisky largely goes into blends, although some producers do bottle single grains.

In crude terms, single malts tend to be more expensive than blends, but this isn't necessarily a reflection of quality, as an individual might prefer the

An advertisement for Teacher's Scotch Whisky and Grand Liqueur in the 1901 edition of Scotland's Industrial Souvenir

complexity and character of a particular blend and blending is an art in itself. For example, a blended Scotch whisky might be a mix of up to 50 individual malt and grain whiskies from a number of distilleries. Skilful mixing by the blender maintains the consistency and quality of the whisky. The age of the blend is taken as the age of the youngest whisky in the mix.

Scotch whisky, which is spelt without the letter e, must be made in Scotland, is generally double-distilled, although there are exceptions, and is matured for at least three years. Whiskey made elsewhere in the world, including North America, is spelt with the e.

It's hard to give an ABV (alcohol by volume) for whisky or whiskey, but the standard is at least 40 per cent. The classic way to drink most quality whiskies is neat, with ice and or water to taste, although purists would say the taste is ruined by adding water. They would add that if a drinker insists on diluting a Scotch whisky, they should do it with still Scottish mineral water, ideally the same water used to make that specific whisky, rather than chlorine-laden tap water, but that might prove tricky. Whiskies are also often mixed with soda water, ginger ale or commonly cola, and are used in many cocktails.

SCOTCH WHISKY BRANDS

❖ **Glenfiddich** is a single malt Scotch whisky produced in the region of Speyside. The whisky is bottled at 12, 15, 18, 21, 30, 40 and 50 years old.

❖ **Glenlivet** is a single malt also produced in Speyside. The standard is the 12-year-old, which is aged in oak, which gives it a vanilla sweetness.

❖ **Glenmorangie** is a single malt produced in the Highlands. The water local to most Scottish distilleries is soft, but Glenmorangie's water rises up through limestone and is quite hard, and this adds to its particular taste. As well as a ten-year-old and other vintage editions, Glenmorangie produces whisky with a sherry finish, which has been aged in

old sherry casks, a madeira finish, a burgundy finish and so on.

❖ **Highland Park** is a single malt from Scotland's most northerly distillery, Kirkwall in the Orkney Islands. The distillery still malts its own barley using Orkney peat which gives the whisky a heathery aroma. The standard bottling is a 12-year-old.

❖ **Lagavulin** is a single malt produced on the island of Islay, in the Western Isles, a short hop from Ireland. The 16-year-old is the standard and it has an ABV of 40 per cent and a smoky, peaty flavour.

❖ **Laphroaig** is a single malt produced at a 200-year-old distillery, also on the isle of Islay, in ten-, 15-, 30- and even 40-year-old editions.

❖ **Talisker** is a single malt produced on the island of Skye, in the Inner Hebrides, using water from 14 underground springs. The ten-year-old has an ABV of 45.8 per cent.

❖ **The Macallan** is a single malt from the Highlands. The company offers a wide range of whiskies of different ages, including a rather expensive Macallan 1861 Replica, which gives the drinker a good sense of what a 19th-century-style malt would have tasted like.

Popular brands of blended Scotch whisky include Bell's, Chivas Regal, Johnnie Walker, Teacher's Highland Cream and The Famous Grouse.

IRISH WHISKEY

In many ways, Irish whiskey is similar to Scotch whisky, but there are distinct differences in taste. For example, in Ireland barley is rarely malted over a peat fire, so Irish whiskey doesn't have the smokiness of Scotch.

The basic process for making Irish whiskey is much the same as that used to make Scotch whisky, but Irish whiskey tends to contain malted barley plus a wider range of grains and it is usually triple-distilled in pot stills. Like Scotch whisky, it must be aged for at least three years. To be described as Irish whiskey, a spirit must also be distilled and matured in Ireland.

IRISH WHISKEY BRANDS

❖ **Bushmills** is a well-known brand of Irish whiskey. The company produces a ten-year-old and a 16-year-old malt, as well as the Black Bush blend.

❖ **Jameson** is another well-known brand of Irish whiskey. The blend is produced from 50 per cent grain whiskey and 50 per cent malt, aged in old bourbon casks for smoothness, with 10 per cent in sherry casks for richness.

BOURBON

Bourbon is a whiskey that must be produced in the USA from a grain mash of not less than 51 per cent corn (maize) and aged for at least two years in new barrels that have been charred inside. It is a sour mash whiskey, which means that spent mash left over from the previous fermentation is added to each new batch. The name bourbon comes from Bourbon County in Kentucky (ironically the only 'dry' county in the state), but the drink can be made anywhere in the States.

Well-known brands of bourbon include Jim Beam, with an ABV of 40 per cent, Maker's Mark, which has an ABV of 45 per cent, or 50.5 per cent in certain export markets, and Wild Turkey, which has an ABV of 50.5 per cent.

RYE WHISKEY

Made mostly in North America, the basic process for making rye whiskey, or simply rye, is similar to that used for making Scotch whisky and Irish whiskey. However, in the United States, rye whiskey must be

produced from a grain mash made up of at least 51 per cent rye grain and aged in new barrels that have been charred inside, while in Canada the only stipulation is that the beverage must be made in Canada. Rye whiskey is not usually as sweet as bourbon and the rye tends to give it a slight pepperiness.

TENNESSEE WHISKEY

Like bourbon, Tennessee whiskey is a sour mash whiskey, but it differs from bourbon in that it is filtered through maple charcoal before it is aged. There are no regulations governing exactly how Tennessee whiskey must be made.

Jack Daniel's is a well-known brand of Tennessee whiskey, which is sold in distinctive rectangular bottles with a black label. It has an ABV of 40 per cent. It is drunk straight, with ice, in mixed drinks, particularly with cola, and is an ingredient in several cocktails. Jack Daniel's is a brand with a loyal following and Frank Sinatra was allegedly buried with a flask of it by his side.

WHISKY/WHISKEY LIQUEURS

❖ **Drambuie** is a Scottish liqueur made from whisky flavoured with heather, honey and herbs.
❖ **Glayva**, another Scottish whisky-based liqueur, has similar flavours, but with the addition of citrus fruits.
❖ **Baileys Irish Cream** is an Irish whiskey and cream-based liqueur – indeed the original cream liqueur – with chocolate flavouring and an ABV of 15 per cent. It is now available with a hint of mint or a dash of caramel too.
❖ **Sheridan's** is another Irish whiskey-based liqueur. It comes in a distinctive bottle that's divided into two sections, one containing a dark whiskey-based coffee liqueur, the other a creamy white liqueur. To serve, pour the dark liquid first and float the light one on top.

❖ **Irish Mist** is also a whiskey-based liqueur.
It is flavoured with herbs and heather honey.

❖ **Southern Comfort** is a brand of American
whiskey-based liqueur, flavoured with, among
other ingredients, peach brandy, orange, vanilla
and cinnamon, and available in a range of
different ABVs. It can be mixed with soda water
or cola and is used in a number of cocktails.

HOMEBREWS

Irish homebrew spirit is called poteen. It is usually
distilled from grain or potatoes and has the highest
ABV of any drink in the world – according to legend at
least. Poteen, which is often rather rough, was banned

in Ireland for more than two centuries, but legalised in the late 1990s, although commercial versions tend to have a more moderate ABV than the bathtub stuff. There are many variant spellings of poteen, including poitin, potheen and potcheen.

In the USA, illegally distilled homebrew whiskey, which is often fairly rough, is known as moonshine.

VODKA

Popular all over the world, but with its origins in Russia (the Russians believe they invented it, but this is disputed), central and eastern Europe (the Polish also claim they invented it) and Scandinavia, vodka is a clear spirit once used for medicinal purposes.

Vodka can be distilled from pretty much any plant matter that contains a lot of sugar and can be fermented, including potatoes, sugar beet and soya beans. Today most commercial vodka is made from a mash of grains such as wheat, rye or corn and filtered through charcoal. It has an ABV that can range from 35 to 50 per cent. Although it isn't usually aged, vodka is often flavoured or sometimes coloured with fruits such as lemon or cranberry, or spices such as pepper.

Vodka has the excellent attribute that you can't detect it on the drinker's breath and this neutrality makes it an important ingredient in many classic cocktails.

VODKA BRANDS

❖ **42 Below** is a 42 per cent ABV vodka from New Zealand, available flavoured with kiwi, passion fruit, manuka honey or a native fruit called feijoa.

❖ **Absolut Vodka** is a famous Swedish brand of vodka, distilled in Ahus in southern Sweden from local wheat grain and then filtered through charcoal. Absolut Blue has an ABV of 40 per cent and there are various flavours available, including Citron (lemon), Kurant (blackcurrant) and Peppar (jalapenos and green tomatoes).

❖ **Bison Grass** is a brand of Polish vodka. It's made in a style called zubrowka and flavoured with a plant called bison grass – an alleged aphrodisiac – which gives it a yellowy colour. Every bottle contains a single blade of bison grass. Like other vodkas, Bison Grass is usually served chilled, but Poles mix it with apple juice, although outside Poland it's sometimes mixed with Red Bull for a double bovine hit.

❖ **Finlandia** is a 40 per cent ABV brand of vodka made in Finland, available in several flavours, including cranberry and mango.

❖ **Grey Goose** You don't tend to think of the French as vodka-makers, but this brand is produced in the Cognac region of France.

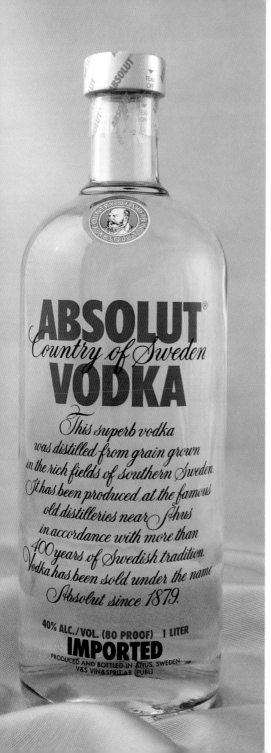

❖ **Reyka** is a small-batch Icelandic vodka filtered
through lava rock at a distillery powered by
geothermal steam.

❖ **Smirnoff** is a Russian vodka, which claims it was
the first to be filtered through charcoal and has
several variants, including the pre-mixed alcopop
Smirnoff Ice, which is flavoured with citrus.

❖ **Stolichnaya** is a Russian vodka made from winter
wheat and Siberian glacial water, available in several
flavours, including strawberry and raspberry. The
Red Label version has an ABV of 40 per cent.

❖ **Wyborowa** vodka is made in Poznan, Poland, using
rye from the local area and water from an ancient
local well.

GIN

This is a spirit distilled from any grain, potato or
beet, flavoured with juniper and other herbs, and

usually redistilled. It originated in Holland in the 17th century, but quickly became popular in England and by the 18th century it was so cheap it was more widely consumed than beer, even though it was commonly flavoured with turpentine. As a consequence, gin was blamed for a range of social ills – as illustrated by the slang name, 'mother's ruin' – and for London's rising death rate. In 1736 and 1751 the government passed Gin Acts to tax gin retail sales and bring them under control. Despite the odd riot, this was eventually achieved, although illicit gin stills continued to produce gin for an eager black market. By the 20th century gin had managed to shake off its plebian roots and is now a spirit of some sophistication. It is usually drunk with ice and a slice of lemon, and is the base for numerous cocktails, including a straightforward gin and tonic and a martini.

GIN TYPES AND BRANDS

❖ **London dry gin** was originally a gin produced in or near London, but is now a very dry gin, with an ABV of around 40 per cent, that is produced anywhere. Well-known brands of London dry gin include Beefeater, Bombay Sapphire, Gilbey's, Gordon's, which holds the Royal Warrant for gin, and Tanqueray.

❖ **Hendrick's** is a brand of gin made in Scotland. It also has an ABV of 40 per cent, but boasts an unusual additional flavouring in the form of cucumber – the producer suggests it is served with a slice of that instead of lemon or lime.

❖ **Plymouth gin** is a brand of gin produced in Plymouth, Devon – the standard gin has an ABV of 41 per cent and the Navy Strength version an ABV of 57 per cent.

❖ **Old Tom** is a sweetened American gin used primarily in cocktails.

❖ **Sloe gin** is a sweetened gin infused with sloes, the fruit of the blackthorn bush.

Sloe gin is really easy to make at home. Pick your sloes from blackthorn hedges in October or November when they are most ripe – probably after the first frosts. Take a half-full litre bottle of gin. Cut or prick the sloes and drop into the half-empty bottle so that they displace the remaining gin to near the top. Add approximately 150 g of sugar. All you have to do now is turn or agitate the bottle daily for a week, then weekly for a month or two ... by which time it will be ready to drink (but it is really best kept until the next winter).

SCHNAPPS

Schnapps is something of a catch-all term. In Germany, Austria and Switzerland it is called schnaps or sometimes korn, and is a spirit or fruit brandy distilled from fermented grain or fruit, commonly apple, pear, plum and so on, but unsweetened. This is a crucial point of difference between a schnapps and a liqueur. In Scandinavia, the drink snaps or aquavit, usually distilled from grain or potatoes, possibly flavoured, but certainly not sweetened, is equivalent to schnapps. In all these places, schnapps is drunk neat, chilled, in small shots, during the course of a meal, sometimes accompanied by a fulsome toast.

Generally clear and somewhat similar in taste to vodka, schnapps has an ABV of around 40 per cent or a little lower if it is fruity. However, it isn't drunk very much in the UK, with Archers, which is flavoured with peaches, one of the few widely available brands. Another is a Swiss schnapps called Goldschlager, which is flavoured with cinnamon and has little flakes of real gold floating in it.

Just to add to the confusion, in the United States the word schnapps usually refers to what would be called a liqueur in the UK.

AQUAVIT

A clear or pale yellow Scandinavian spirit distilled from fermented grain or potatoes and flavoured with cardamon, cumin, fennel and particularly caraway seeds. Aquavit is drunk straight and chilled, often with an appetiser of pickled or smoked fish, and has an ABV of around 40 per cent. The name, which is sometimes spelt akvavit, comes from the Latin for water of life (*aqua vitae*).

Around 15 types of akvavit are made in the Jutland town of Aalborg, which is the indisputable capital of the Danish akvavit industry.

DRINKS DISTILLED FROM GRAPES

WINE

One of the most widely consumed drinks in the world, at its most simple wine is no more than fermented grape juice and it has been made in Europe and the Middle East since around 5,000 BC. However, wine is also an extensive and complicated topic that can take years to master and the modern wine-making process is extremely sophisticated.

In essence, though, the crushed grapes (must) or pressed grapes (juice) are fermented for a couple of weeks. If the grapes don't contain enough of their own yeast for fermentation, cultured yeast is added. During this time the vast majority of the natural sugars turn into alcohol (ethanol). Then the remaining sugars are left to change into alcohol more slowly over a period of three to six months. Some wines are then bottled, while others are aged further in wooden casks.

Red wine is made from red or black grapes, but the colour comes from the skins, which are left on during fermentation. White wine can be made from any colour of grape, as long as the skins are separated and only the juice is used. Rosé is made by removing the dark grape skins in the middle of the fermentation process, or by blending red and white wine.

Wines can be described on a scale of dry through to sweet, depending on how much natural sugar is left after the fermentation process. Even where one grape variety is dominant, most wines are blends of two or more varieties. Vintage wines are made from grapes that were all grown in a single year and are labelled with that date. Some vintages are inevitably better than others. Table wines normally contain between 10 per cent and 14 per cent ABV.

How a wine actually tastes depends on a range of factors, from the type of grape, the earth or *terroir* the vine grows in, the weather in any one growing season, the choice of actual grapes, the fermentation process, how long and in what a wine is aged before it is bottled and how long it is kept before it is drunk.

The French are major wine-makers and classic fine wines have traditionally come from France, which controls and classifies its wine production with a rigorous *Appellation* system – from *vin de table*, which must be from France, through *vin de pays*, which has to be from a named region of France, up to *Appellation d'Origine Contrôlée*, which indicates wine from a specific area, produced to certain rules. Italy, Spain, Portugal and many other European countries are notable wine-producers, and wine from Australia, New Zealand, the United States, South Africa, Argentina and Chile – known as 'new world' wine – is now popular around the globe.

Old world wines from Europe tend to be named after the area in which they were produced and their main constituent grape. New world wines tend to be named after their predominant grape variety, although this is changing as the character of the area from which a wine comes is seen to be increasingly important.

In general, white wines are served slightly chilled, while red wines are served at room temperature but, of course, there are exceptions to these rules.

NATIONAL WINES

❖ **French** wine is often assumed – especially by the French – to be the best in the world, but with the rise of new world wines from Australia, the United States and South America, its position of pre-eminence has been threatened. However, the best French wines are still the benchmark against which other wines are judged and many French wine-producing regions are household names.

Bordeaux, for example, is a famous wine-growing region in south-west France, which produces the fine reds: Graves, Médoc, Pomerol and Saint-Emilion, as well as the dessert wine Sauternes. Claret is the name given to the red wines of Bordeaux, particularly those from the Medoc. Burgundy is another famous wine-growing region. It is situated south of Paris and includes the sub-region Chablis, which produces predominantly chardonnay-based whites, and Beaujolais, known for its gamay-based reds. Beaujolais nouveau is the first bottling of the Beaujolais harvest, released annually to the public at midnight on the third Thursday in November – a time-honoured marketing ploy. Burgundy's Côte de Nuits and Côte de Beaune produce some of the world's finest red wines, based on the difficult-to-cultivate pinot noir grape.

❖ **Italian** wine is made in most regions of the country, as grapes grow just about everywhere in Italy, and it can boast many famous labels, including Chianti, Barolo and Valpolicella, all of which are red, and Soave, which is white. Wines based on the white pinot grigio grape are also made in several regions and are increasingly popular internationally. Prosecco is a naturally fermented Italian white sparkling wine from Veneto, which takes its name from the prosecco grape variety, while Asti (the Spumante has been dropped from its name), also naturally fermented, is a sweet sparkler from Piedmont that's often drunk with dessert. The Italian system of wine classification and regulation has four categories, the top two of which are *Denominazione di Origine Controllata* and *Denominazione di Origine Controllata e Garantita*.

❖ **Spanish** wine is made in 50 recognised wine regions and Spain produces high-quality reds from Rioja and Ribera del Duero, fine whites from Rueda, and reds and whites from Penedes. Spanish sparkling wine is known as cava and Spain also produces the famous fortified wine sherry. Its *Denominación de Origen* system classifies and regulates wine production.

❖ **Portuguese** wine includes some good table wines, particularly the reds from Douro in the north, all classified and regulated according to its *Denominação de Origem Controlada* system. However, Portugal is best known for its fortified wines: port and madeira.

❖ **German** wine and the German wine industry were dominant in the 19th century, but their current reputation is for cheap and unchallenging sweet white wines – in other words Liebfraumilch. However, that is beginning to change and some of the country's smaller, and formerly great, producers are now endeavouring to produce high quality, more imaginative wines, many of them based on the white riesling grape. One of these is the unusual Eiswein, a sweet German wine made from grapes left on the vine until the first frosts come – the word means 'ice wine'. Similar high-quality wines are also produced in Austria.

❖ **English** wine has a long history, as vines have been grown in England since Roman times and, although the English wine industry consists of about 400 small vineyards with a correspondingly small output principally of white wine, the quality of at least some of its products has certainly improved over

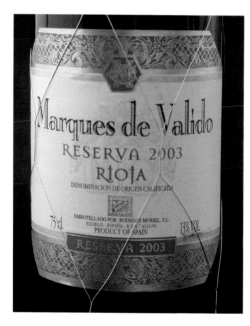

Some Spanish wines, particularly Riojas, come in bottles with a thin wire wrapped around them. This practice first became popular during the war to stop people from opening the bottles and replacing the wine with an inferior one. Today it is more of a marketing exercise.

the last few decades, and English wines are enjoyed and indeed feted in some quarters. English wine, however, should be distinguished from British wine, which is usually made from imported concentrates and is not known for its high price or quality.

❖ **Australian** wines have only really become popular in the UK in the last couple of decades, but the country has been producing wine for over 200 years and has several world-class wine-growing regions, predominantly in the south-east of the country, including the Barossa and Hunter Valleys, and Coonawarra. The reputation of 'new world' Australian wines was founded on big, full-bodied reds from grapes such as Cabernet Sauvignon and Shiraz (Syrah in Europe), but today most of the world's major grape varieties are grown and most styles are produced, including acclaimed sparkling wine and dessert wine.

❖ **New Zealand** wine has one really big name – the much-in-demand, intense, Cloudy Bay sauvignon blanc – but it also produces good white chardonnays and rieslings, and the country's cool maritime climate encourages the production of some fine red pinot noirs.

❖ **American** wine is almost all made in California, including the big red cabernet sauvignons of the Napa Valley and Sonoma, and the pinot noir of the Santa Ynez Valley, as popularised by the film *Sideways*, but other states, such as Oregon and Washington, are also producers.

❖ **Argentinian** wine, the good stuff anyway, is mostly exported, while the not-so-good stuff is kept for home consumption. The country's own grape variety, Malbec, is used to make some of its strong reds, and Torrontes, also specific to Argentina, is used for some of its whites.

❖ **Chilean** wine is also successfully exported and the country's top-quality products include those made with Carmenère, the country's own red grape variety.

❖ **South African** wine is traditionally white and based on the chenin blanc grape, but as the South

African wine industry matures it is increasingly successful at turning out good quality reds. There are a number of wine-growing areas, but Stellenbosch is probably the best-known.

CHAMPAGNE

Quite simply the most famous French wine-growing region in the world, Champagne specialises in wine that undergoes its second fermentation in the bottle. The resulting product contains bubbles of carbon dioxide that give it a fizz.

When opening a bottle of champagne, aim for a soft pop rather than a bang as the cork comes out. The current fashion is for serving champagne in a champagne flute, which is tall and narrow, so the bubbles and aroma are retained. Tilt the glass slightly and pour the chilled bubbly on to the side of the glass, until it's three-quarters full.

Well-known brands of champagne include Bollinger, abbreviated by those who drink it frequently to Bolly; Krug; Louis Roederer, producer of the luxury vintage champagne Cristal, famously guzzled by celebrities; Moet & Chandon, whose brands include the luxury champagne Dom Perignon, which is only produced in years when the vintage is exceptional; Pol Roger; Taittinger and Veuve Clicquot.

Countries other than France produce fizzy or sparkling wine, but they're not allowed to call it champagne as the French have sought to protect the name legally. In Spain it's cava, in Italy it's asti, in Germany and Austria it's sekt, and in the rest of France outside the Champagne region it's cremant. Most sparkling wines are white, with Australia producing some sparkling reds and California well-known for its rosés. However, in less expensive products the sparkle may have been added by injection, rather than in-bottle fermentation.

SHERRY

In order to carry the name sherry, this Spanish fortified wine must be produced in a triangular area formed by the three Andalucian towns of El Puerto de Santa Maria, Sanlucar de Barrameda and Jerez de la Frontera – the word sherry is a corruption of 'Jerez'.

Versions of sherry have long been produced in the region. Because it is fortified, sherry tends to travel better than unfortified wine and it has been exported to the UK since the 12th century. As a consequence, many of the sherry-making establishments, or 'bodegas', were founded by British families in the late 17th and early 18th centuries.

To make sherry, wine is fortified with brandy and then, for a pale fino sherry, a yeast called flor is encouraged to grow on top to give flavour. Manzanilla is a light fino sherry that comes exclusively from Sanlucar de Barrameda.

Amontillado sherry is made in the same way, but after the flor has died, it is exposed to the air. This produces

with Pedro Ximenez, and the fino Tio Pepe. In the United States sherry is used as a generic term for fortified wine, but must be labelled with its state of origin, for example Californian sherry.

PORT

Made in the Douro river valley in northern Portugal and exported through the nearby port of Porto, from whence it obviously gets its name, port is a red wine that is fortified by the addition of brandy, giving it an ABV of around 20 per cent.

Port has always been well liked in the UK. This dates back to the late 17th century and early 18th century, when England was at war with France. This meant the English weren't able to get their hands on any French wine, but the government lowered the import duty on Portuguese wine and it became inexpensive and thus very popular in England. However, on the long journey by sea from Portugal to England the wine often spoiled, so the shippers began to add brandy to stabilise it and extend its shelf life. Eventually, instead of being added just before it was shipped, the brandy began to be added during the fermentation process and port was created.

Port is traditionally an after-dinner drink and is often partnered with cheese, especially Stilton. The best quality port is vintage port, which is made from the grapes of a single year's harvest, although not every year is deemed good enough to be declared a vintage. Vintage port tends to be unfiltered, so it does need to be decanted before drinking to remove the sediment, and it should be served at room temperature.

Ruby port is a fruity, young, deep red-coloured port, a blend of wine from several different harvests that's usually aged for two or three years before being bottled. Tawny port is either aged a lot longer than Ruby port, until it takes on a golden-brown colour and a more mellow, nutty taste, or it is made from lighter wines which give it a tawny appearance. Late Bottled Vintage, or LBV, is made from a single year and bottled between

a slightly darker liquid. Oloroso sherry is oxidised for even longer, resulting in an even darker product. What is called medium sherry is usually sweetened amontillado, while sweet sherry is sweetened oloroso. Palo cortado is a rare style of dry sherry, with a character halfway between an amontillado and an oloroso, which is produced when the flor or yeast fails to develop fully. Cream and pale cream sherries are usually sweetened blends of one or more of the three types of sherry. The sweetening is done with wine made from locally grown Pedro Ximenez or Moscatel grapes.

Sherry is drunk as an aperitif or sometimes as an after-dinner drink. It is essentially a white wine, so it should be served lightly chilled, although sweet dessert sherries are best at room temperature.

Well-known brands of sherry include the pale cream Croft Original, Harveys Bristol Cream, which is made from a mix of fino, amontillado and oloroso sweetened

The finest vintage ports are blended using wine of the same year from the finest vineyards. The port is then aged in barrels for a maximum of two and a half years before bottling. They generally require another ten to thirty years of ageing in the bottle before reaching what is considered a proper drinking age.

four and six years. White port is made from white grapes, has a lighter, fresher taste and isn't aged. It is usually drunk chilled, as an aperitif.

Port has many rituals associated with it. For example, in the olden days, at the end of a meal the ladies would retire and the gentlemen would pass a decanter of port around the table, but always to the person on the left of them. Anyone who kept the decanter in front of them for too long would be accused of being the Bishop of Norwich, after a greedy cleric of yore. If you wanted someone to pass the port to you, you asked whether the person hogging it knew the Bishop of Norwich. If they misunderstood and said no, you would reply that he was an awfully nice man, but never passed the port.

Well-known brands of vintage port include Dow, Sandeman and Taylor.

MADEIRA

Like its close cousin port, madeira is a Portuguese fortified wine, although it isn't made on the mainland but on the island of Madeira, which lies in the Atlantic, over 500 miles from the Portuguese capital Lisbon. Again like port, Madeira is fortified with brandy, which was first added to help the wine survive long sea voyages, but unlike vintage port it is matured at high temperatures and oxidised, which gives it more mellow taste and a golden-brown colour not dissimilar to that of tawny port. Madeira is a pleasant drink that should be served at room temperature, perhaps accompanied by a slice of madeira sponge cake, which doesn't usually contain madeira, but which was invented in the UK specifically for this purpose.

wine is boiled in a still until the water and alcohol turn to vapour. The vapours are then collected and condensed, so that they turn back into a liquid with a high alcohol content. This is then aged, usually in oak barrels, and eventually diluted to between 40 and 60 per cent ABV. There's a grading system related to how long brandy is aged, in which VS (Very Special) indicates a product has been aged for at least three years, VSOP (Very Superior Old Pale) means five years, XO (Extra Old) is six years and Hors D'age roughly ten years.

Brandy has been made in Armagnac for longer than it has been made in Cognac, and the wines used in both regions are largely from the same varieties of grape, but in Cognac the brandy is distilled twice, while in Armagnac it is almost always distilled just once. In exceptionally crude terms, this results in armagnac being more 'gutsy' and cognac being more 'refined' on the palate.

BRANDY

The name comes from the Dutch for burnt (boiled) wine – *brandewijn* – and brandy is the word for a distilled wine. Distilled wines are produced in many countries, including Spain, Portugal, Germany, South Africa and the United States, but 'real' brandy comes from one of two *Appellation d'Origine Contrôlée* regions in France – Armagnac, in south-western France in the foothills of the Pyrenees, and Cognac, in western France on the Atlantic coast.

Although the ancient Greeks and Romans distilled alcohol, brandy as it is drunk today first appeared in the 12th century and became popular in Europe round about the 14th century. Very simply, to make brandy,

Brandy generally has a caramel colour, due to the effect of ageing in wooden casks or, in less expensive examples, the addition of a caramel colourant. Although essentially an after-dinner drink, when it is drunk neat, at room temperature, brandy is also a vital ingredient for many cocktails and indeed younger brandies are perfect for this purpose.

BRANDY BRANDS

❖ **Janneau** is a popular brand of armagnac, although the company has departed from tradition and uses a double-distillation process that was formerly the hallmark of rival cognac-producers. Its range includes five-, eight- and 15-year-old brandies, as well as single vintages.
❖ **Courvoisier** is a popular brand of cognac. The Courvoisier company boasts a strong connection with Napoleons I and III, and produces a range of products at varying levels. Courvoisier VSOP Exclusif, for example, is designed to be mixed.
❖ **Hennessy** is another popular brand of cognac and the preferred tipple of many rap artists, certainly judging by the number of times it's name-checked in their lyrics. The product ranges from a standard VS through to an ultra-expensive Ellipse, of which only a hundred bottles are produced annually.
❖ **Hine Rare VSOP** is blended from over 25 different cognacs, the youngest of which is at least four years old, as it must be to qualify for the VSOP designation. Hine Antique XO contains over 40 cognacs, the youngest of which is at least six years old.
❖ **Martell VS** is a cognac blend that's aged for two years and, at the other end of the company's range, Martell L'Or includes cognacs aged in barrels for more than 60 years.
❖ **Remy Martin VSOP** is aged in unusually small oak barrels that intensify the effects of the ageing process.

OTHER BRANDY TYPES AND LIQUEURS

❖ **Marc** is a rather harsh French brandy distilled from the fermented pulp, skins and stalks left behind after the grape juice is extracted for wine.
❖ **Grappa**, the Italian version – made in roughly the same way – ranges from the eye-wateringly rough to a sophisticated spirit from a particular grape variety.
❖ **Aguardiente**, which translates as 'burning water' or 'firewater', is the generic Spanish name for a brandy with an ABV of between 30 and 45 per cent. In Portugal the same spirit is called aguardente. In Chile aguardiente is distilled grape skins and pulp, similar to marc or grappa, but in Brazil, Colombia and Mexico it's something different – a sugar cane spirit or rum.
❖ **Fruit brandy** is also a different thing. This is the generic term for a brandy distilled from wine made from a fruit other than grapes.
❖ **Advocaat** is a Dutch liqueur made of egg yolks and sugar mixed with a brandy base and often flavoured with vanilla. Advocaat is bright yellow and has a creamy consistency. Its ABV is usually between 15 and 20 per cent and it is the principal ingredient in a Snowball. Famous advocaat-makers include Bols and Warninks.
❖ **Alizé** At 16 per cent ABV, this relatively low-alcohol liqueur is a blend of cognac, vodka and fruit juice. It comes in Gold Passion (passion fruit), Red Passion (cranberry and peach), Wild Passion (pink grapefruit and mango), Bleu (cherry and ginger) and Rose (rose, strawberry and lychee, but no cognac) versions.

VERMOUTH

Whatever variation you favour, vermouth is an essential ingredient of a Martini. A fortified wine with an ABV of between 15 and 18 per cent, the red version was invented in 18th-century Italy by one Antonio Benedetto Carpano, but the French developed a white version in the 19th century.

There are basically three types of vermouth. Red or rosso vermouth is rather sweet and is drunk neat as an aperitif or with a mixer. Bianco is, as you would expect, white and not quite as sweet as the red. Dry vermouth is also white and, well, quite dry. This is the one to use in a Martini. Although the red is sometimes known as Italian vermouth and the white as French vermouth, in practice all styles are now made by both Italian and French producers.

The name comes from the German *wermut*, meaning wormwood, which is one of the herbs used to flavour vermouth and which is indeed the crucial mind-altering component in absinthe. Vermouth contains only a tiny amount of wormwood, however, along with a range of other herbs and spices, the precise list depending on each producer's own secret recipe. The flavourings were originally used to disguise the taste of the cheap wine base. The fortification in today's commercial products is usually courtesy of a grape-based spirit.

Dry vermouth should be refrigerated and will keep for about six months. Other vermouths will last a year as long as they're stored in a cool place.

VERMOUTH BRANDS

❖ **Cinzano** is a well-known brand of Italian vermouth. Anyone watching TV in the 1980s will remember the ad with Joan Collins and Leonard Rossiter on a plane…

❖ **Dubonnet** is a well-known brand of French vermouth, flavoured with quinine and bitter bark, and with an ABV of 17 per cent.

❖ **Martini & Rossi** is a well-known brand of Italian vermouth. Although the firm is named after one of its founders, some say the name of the cocktail, in which vermouth is a vital ingredient, comes from the same source, but there are also several other stories about why a Martini is called a Martini.

❖ **Noilly Prat** is a well-known brand of French vermouth, flavoured with around 20 herbs and spices and with an ABV of 17 per cent.

DRINKS FLAVOURED WITH HERBS AND SPICES

ANGOSTURA BITTERS

Angostura bitters is made from a secret blend of herbs and spices and is best described as a concentrated flavouring. Despite its name, it isn't bitter when added to a drink, and has the ability to bring out the flavour of the other ingredients. It was invented in the 19th century by an army doctor in Venezuela who used it to improve the appetite of his soldiers, but it is now produced in Trinidad. It has a high ABV of 44.7 per cent, but recipes rarely call for more than a couple of splashes of it. Angostura has a distinctive label that's too big for the bottle – apparently an error that nobody got round to rectifying – and it is what makes a Pink Gin, which is simply gin and Angostura bitters, pink.

PIMM'S

Pimm's was invented in the early 19th century by James Pimm, the proprietor of a City of London oyster bar, and Pimm's No. 1 Cup is a fruity, gin-based drink flavoured with a secret mix of herbs. Although originally sold as an aid to digestion, Pimm's, which is the colour of strong tea with a pinky blush, is a quintessentially English summer drink.

The traditional way to serve Pimm's No. 1 is to mix up a pitcher of one part Pimm's to two parts lemonade and add a veritable fruit cocktail of orange, lemon, apple and cucumber slices, plus a few sprigs of mint and ice. However, Pimm's is also used in a range of other cocktail recipes.

At one time there was a range of Pimm's drinks numbering one to six, each based on a different spirit,

The recipe for Angostura bitters was developed in 1824 by Dr Johann Gottlieb Benjamin Siegert, a surgeon in Simon Bolívar's army. He was based in Ciudad Bolívar in Venezuela, which was then known as Angostura, and used locally available ingredients.

By the late 19th century absinthe had become associated with Parisian artists and writers, but it was also thought to be dangerously addictive and was blamed for a variety of social ills, including violent crime. Consequently, in 1915 it was banned in France. However, by the late 20th century the European Union relaxed the ban and absinthe has since enjoyed a revival, although it remains illegal to produce and sell, although not to consume, absinthe in the United States.

The classic way to prepare absinthe is to place a sugar cube on a spoon over a glass, then pour a slug of absinthe over the sugar cube and set light to it. When the sugar has melted and dripped into the glass, add ice-cold water (three to five parts to one part absinthe) to douse the flames and to taste. Diluting absinthe causes it to go cloudy. This is known as louching.

but these were dropped in the 1970s and in addition to No. 1 the only other Pimm's now available is the No. 3, which carries the sobriquet Winter, is based on brandy and has a spicier, more orangey taste. Both Pimm's No. 1 and No. 3 have an ABV of 25 per cent.

ABSINTHE

Absinthe derives its name from the Latin for wormwood (*Artemesia absinthium*) and this spirit is distilled from a mix of bitter herbs, including wormwood, aniseed, angelica and cloves. Legend has it that a Frenchman called Dr Ordiniare invented absinthe as a patent remedy sometime in the late 18th century. Its greeny-yellowish colour – and some would say its taste – are certainly somewhat medicinal, but it is a highly alcoholic spirit, which can range from 50 to 90 per cent ABV, and its effects are far more likely to be detrimental than beneficial to the drinker's health.

Also known as green fairy and la fée, in Italy absinthe is called assenzio, in Spain it's ajenjo, and in Morocco it's chiba. Such is the glamour and mystique surrounding absinthe that there are various specialised pieces of equipment available, including slotted absinthe spoons.

LILLET

Lillet is a French fortified wine, available in red and white, and flavoured with herbs and fruit.

MEAD

Mead is fermented honey and water often flavoured with a few herbs, and it's always cited as the oldest drink known to humankind.

WORCESTERSHIRE SAUCE

Worcestershire sauce is a fermented spicy sauce containing, among other ingredients, vinegar, molasses (treacle) and anchovies. It is often used to liven up a Bloody Mary. The best-known brand is Lee & Perrins Worcestershire sauce.

TABASCO

Tabasco is a hot pepper sauce made from tabasco peppers. It's often used to put a kick into a Bloody Mary too.

LIQUEURS FLAVOURED WITH HERBS AND SPICES

❖ **Chartreuse** is a French liqueur flavoured with herbs and originally made by monks. As with many

of the old herb liqueurs, the exact recipe is top secret and allegedly only the three monks who prepare the herbal mixture are in possession of it. Green chartreuse is bright green and has an ABV of 55 per cent, while yellow chartreuse has an ABV of 40 per cent and is sweeter. The yellowy-green colour chartreuse is named after the drink.

❖ **Benedictine** was developed in the 16th century by a Benedictine monk called Dom Bernardo Vincelli at an abbey in Normandy, France and this is a cognac-based liqueur flavoured with herbs. As with many similar liqueurs, the exact recipe is a closely guarded secret and it's said that only three people

Tabasco sauce is made from tabasco peppers, vinegar and salt, and aged in white oak barrels for three years. The peppers are grown on Avery Island in Louisiana, USA, as well as in Central and South America, and are hand picked to ensure they are ripe. Tabasco has been produced by the McIlhenny Company since 1868.

know it at any one time. The company that owns the Benedictine brand also produces a liqueur called B and B, in which Benedictine is further diluted with brandy to make it drier.

❖ **Angelica** is a pale yellow French liqueur of 40 per cent ABV flavoured with the plant angelica and made in the Pyrenees region. There is also a yellow Spanish liqueur of the same name.

❖ **Crème de Noyau** is a French, almond-flavoured liqueur that is white or pink in colour.

❖ **Parfait Amour** is a purple liqueur, mostly made in France and Holland, which usually has a curaçao base, flavoured with vanilla, almonds and rose petal.

❖ **Cuarenta Y Tres** is another yellowy liqueur from Spain. This is flavoured with 43 fruits and herbs, hence the name, which is Spanish for 43. It's also known as Licor 43.

❖ **Amaretto** is a golden-brown Italian liqueur with a bitter/sweet almond taste. Disaronno Originale is a well-known brand of amaretto, which has an ABV of 28 per cent and is flavoured with burnt sugar, and 17 herbs and fruits soaked in apricot kernel oil. Disaronno is made in the Italian town of Saronno, near Lake Como, traces its history back to 1525 and comes in a distinctive square bottle. Amaretto di Amore is another well-known brand of amaretto.

❖ **Fernet Branca** is an Italian herbal liqueur, made from over 40 herbs and spices, which is drunk neat as a digestif, but is also mixed with coffee or cola. It has an ABV of 40 per cent. A mint version called Branca Menta is also available. Strega is also an Italian liqueur flavoured with herbs, including mint and saffron, which gives it a yellow colour. Isolabella is yet another Italian liqueur flavoured with herbs, while Frangelico, also from Italy, gets its taste from herbs and hazelnuts.

❖ **Crème de menthe** is a mint-flavoured liqueur. There are two types, which taste very similar and can be used interchangeably in cocktails, unless the colour is important. The 'white' is clear and the green is coloured with mint leaves or, more usually, an artificial colouring.

❖ **Campari** is an Italian liqueur with an ABV of 25 per cent, which was invented in the 19th century by one Gaspare Campari. As ever, its exact composition is shrouded in mystery, but it contains a bitter mix of around 60 herbs and spices, although sources differ as to what gives it its distinctive red colour – it could be cochineal or it could be capsicum. Either way, campari is traditionally served as an aperitif, neat or with soda water.

❖ **Kümmel** is a clear German, Dutch, sometimes Russian or even Danish liqueur flavoured with caraway. It is also known as kimmel. Underberg is a bitter, herby German digestif, sold in small, single-glass bottles with a distinctive paper wrapper, while Danziger Goldwasser is another German liqueur flavoured with herbs, but distinguished by the small specks of genuine gold floating in it.

❖ **Swedish Punsch** is a Swedish liqueur based on arak and flavoured with various spices, lemon and sugar.

❖ **Metaxa** is a Greek liqueur made of blended brandy and wine and flavoured with herbs.

❖ **Pisang Ambon** is a bright green fruit and herb liqueur with a strong taste of banana, which originated in south-east Asia and is now produced by Dutch company Lucas Bols.

DRINKS FLAVOURED WITH GINGER

❖ **Ginger beer's** origins stretch back to the 18th century and cloudy ginger beer is a quintessentially English summer drink. Mildly fizzy and gently alcoholic, its basic ingredients are ginger, lemon, sugar and a fermenting agent, traditionally something called the ginger beer plant, but equally any other live culture, such as yeast, can be used.

Native to South-East Asia, ginger has long been prized for its aromatic, culinary and medicinal properties. In an attempt to make it more available, Spanish explorers introduced ginger to the West Indies, Mexico and South America in the 16th century, and these areas began exporting the precious herb back to Europe. Today, the top commercial producers of ginger include Jamaica, India, Fiji, Indonesia and Australia.

However, in the United States, ginger beer is often non-alcoholic and more akin to ginger ale, a non-alcoholic, fizzy drink, flavoured with ginger.

❖ **Ginger wine** is a grape-based wine flavoured with ginger and other spices. One of the best-known brands is Stone's Original Green Ginger Wine. This has a history stretching back to the 18th century and has enjoyed steady popularity in the UK. It experienced a particularly strong sales boost during the cholera epidemic of the 1830s, as ginger was believed to offer protection against the disease. It is a 13 per cent ABV fortified grape wine with added ground root ginger and raisins, and as well as being drunk straight it is traditionally splashed into whisky to create a whisky mac. There is also a Special Reserve version with an ABV of 18 per cent. Crabbie's Green Ginger Wine is another well-known brand of ginger wine.

❖ **Falernum** is a sweet, thick, clear syrup used in Caribbean drinks, which contains, among other flavourings, ginger, cloves, lime and sometimes vanilla or allspice. It can be alcoholic or non-alcoholic.

SOFT DRINKS FLAVOURED WITH HERBS

❖ **Cola** is a non-alcoholic, fizzy drink, brown in colour and flavoured with citrus fruits and spices. In common with most soft drinks, cola is drunk on its own, chilled or with ice, but it also mixes well with spirits such as rum or some types of whiskey. Well-known brands include Coca-Cola and Pepsi Cola.

❖ **Rootbeer** is a popular North American non-alcoholic, fizzy drink, which can be flavoured with a variety of roots, berries, barks, plant materials and herbs. It is not dissimilar to the traditional British drinks dandelion and burdock and ginger ale. Alcoholic rootbeers are also available in the United States.

❖ **Dr Pepper** is a well-known brand of non-alcoholic fizzy drink, made to a secret formula of 23 ingredients and coloured with caramel.

DRINKS FLAVOURED WITH ANISEED

PASTIS

Pastis is an aniseed-flavoured liqueur, drunk widely in France, often as an aperitif. Typically it contains 40 to 45 per cent ABV. In 1915, absinthe was banned in France. Facing ruin, absinthe producers re-engineered their potent spirit, removing the wormwood, adding more aniseed and reducing the alcohol, to create pastis. Normally diluted with five parts water, customers like to mix their own, so it is usually served with a jug of iced water. Well-known brands of pastis include Pernod, Ricard and Pastis 51.

RAKI

Raki is often described as the national drink of Turkey, but it's also made elsewhere in central and eastern Europe, and even in the Middle East. Recipes vary, but it is distilled, is generally flavoured with aniseed and tends to be drunk chilled and diluted as an aperitif, perhaps with a plate of meze or hors d'oeuvres. Raki also goes by the names arak or lion's milk.

SAMBUCA

Sambuca is a clear Italian liqueur flavoured with aniseed. It can be drunk neat or with ice and is sometimes served with three coffee beans, representing health, wealth and happiness, floating in it.

GALLIANO

Galliano is a bright yellow Italian liqueur, which is often an ingredient in a Harvey Wallbanger.

JÄGERMEISTER

Jägermeister is a dark red German liqueur flavoured with herbs, including aniseed, and drunk as a digestif.

OUZO

Ouzo is a clear Greek liqueur flavoured with aniseed. It can be drunk straight or with water.

DRINKS MADE FROM CITRUS FRUITS

TRIPLE SEC

Triple sec is a colourless orange-flavoured distilled liqueur used in numerous cocktails as a sweetener, with an ABV of between 15 and 40 per cent.

CURAÇAO

Curaçao is a clear (or white) bitter orange liqueur. It was originally made on the Caribbean island of Curaçao from the bitter peel of the laraha orange, it's now produced in numerous countries and colours, notably green, red, purple and blue, which tends to be the most popular. These exotic hues are achieved by the addition of artificial colouring, but make curaçao extremely useful for cocktails.

GRAND MARNIER

Grand Marnier is a French orange liqueur blended
from cognac and a type of triple sec or curaçao
derived from the bitter, aromatic citrus bigaradia
oranges. The cordon rouge or red ribbon variety is
the original and has an ABV of 40 per cent, while
the cordon jaune or yellow ribbon is of lesser quality.
Grand Marnier can be drunk straight, over ice or
used in cocktails.

COINTREAU

Cointreau is also a clear triple sec or orange liqueur
made from dried bitter orange peel and sweet orange
peel in Angers, France. It has an ABV of 40 per cent
and is commonly served as both an aperitif and a
digestif, but is also used in cocktails.

AURUM

Aurum is a golden, orange-flavoured Italian liqueur with an ABV of 40 per cent, while Tuaca is a brandy-based liqueur from Italy flavoured with vanilla and orange.

LIMONCELLO

Limoncello is a sweet, lemony liqueur from southern Italy. It is not sour, because it is made from lemon peel rather than juice, and a range of alcoholic bases are used. It is usually chilled and served as an after-dinner drink, but it also appears in cocktails.

LEMONADE

Lemonade is a non-alcoholic lemon-flavoured drink made of water, sugar and lemon juice. Commercially produced lemonade, such as 7-Up or Sprite, is usually clear, fizzy and contains both lemon and lime flavouring. This is in contrast to home-made or traditional lemonade, which is cloudy and still, although commercial versions of this type of lemonade, such as Fentimans Victorian Lemonade, may be lightly carbonated. As well as being drunk on its own, chilled or with ice, lemonade mixes well and is added to many cocktails. Bitter lemon – tonic water with added lemon flavouring – is also frequently used as a mixer. Hooper's Hooch is an alcoholic bottled lemonade with an ABV of 4.7 per cent – what is often called an alcopop. Like many lemon- and orange-based drinks it is also available in other fruit flavours.

FRUIT JUICE

Fruit juice is both the unadulterated juice extracted from any fruit, obviously not just citrus fruits, or a drink made from extracted or concentrated juice, sugar and water.

BELVOIR

Belvoir is a brand of non-alcoholic, fruit-based, traditionally styled cordials and pressés (a mix of fruit juice and sparkling mineral water), some of which are organic.

ORANGE BITTERS

Orange bitters is a cocktail flavouring not unlike Angostura bitters, but usually made from the peel of unripe oranges.

DRINKS MADE FROM SOFT OR EXOTIC FRUIT

FRUIT BRANDY

Fruit brandy is the generic term for a brandy distilled from wine made from a fruit other than grapes, as opposed to fruit-flavoured brandy, which is grape wine brandy flavoured with another fruit. Fruit brandy is made all over the world, from a range of fruits, including cherries, apricots and peaches.

KIRSCHWASSER

Kirschwasser is a German fruit brandy made from black cherries, with an ABV of around 40 per cent. Kirschwasser is frequently abbreviated to kirsch and a splash of it is often an ingredient in cheese fondue recipes.

CHERRY HEERING

Cherry Heering is a well-known brandy-based liqueur flavoured with cherries, produced by Danish company Peter Heering.

MIRABELLE

Mirabelle is a French fruit brandy made from plums, with an ABV of around 40 per cent.

QUETSCH

Quetsch is a German fruit brandy distilled from fermented plums, with an ABV of around 40 per cent.

Soft fruits, like cherries, have been served in alcohol since Roman times. The alcohol was first used to preserve the fruit. But their ruby-coloured, soft flesh and deep flavour also complement the acidity of the alcohol and add to its taste.

59

SLIVOVITZ

Slivovitz is an Eastern European and Balkan fruit brandy made from plum wine, with an ABV of around 40 per cent.

PALINKA

Palinka is a Hungarian fruit brandy, usually made from plum wine, but also from other soft fruit wine, with an ABV of around 40 per cent.

LIQUEURS FLAVOURED WITH SOFT OR EXOTIC FRUIT

It's difficult to give a precise definition of the word liqueur, but generally it means a spirit that is flavoured with fruit, herbs or spices and sweetened, although it can also mean a distilled fruit wine. Liqueurs are now made all over the world (somewhat confusingly, in the United States they are known as cordials), but their origins can be traced back to the herbal medicines made by medieval monks.

Although often an after-dinner drink, there are no hard and fast rules about when to serve liqueurs, and likewise they can be consumed straight, with ice or in coffee. They are also an important ingredient in a wide range of cocktails. Many cocktail recipes mix a liqueur with cream, and cream liqueurs, such as Baileys Irish Cream, are now sold ready-mixed as drinks in themselves as well. Crème liqueurs, on the other hand, don't tend to contain real cream and are usually very syrupy liqueurs that have been particularly heavily sweetened. Liqueurs can have an ABV of between 15 and 30 per cent, but some can go as high as 55 per cent ABV.

❖ **Maraschino** is a clear cherry liqueur, made from maraska cherries and their crushed kernels. It has an ABV of around 30 per cent.

❖ **Abricotine** is a yellowy apricot liqueur from France with an ABV of 31.5 per cent. It has a strong almond flavour due to the use of the apricot kernels.

❖ **Midori** is a melon liqueur. It's bright green in colour and has an ABV of 30 per cent.

❖ **Amarula Cream** is a 17 per cent ABV South African liqueur distilled from the wine of the fruit of the marula or elephant tree and mixed with cream.

❖ **Kibowi** is a liqueur made in Holland, flavoured with kiwi fruit.

❖ **Crème de cassis** is a blackcurrant-flavoured liqueur, most commonly used in the cocktails Kir (crème de cassis and white wine) and Kir Royale (crème de cassis and champagne).

❖ **Framboise** is a raspberry-flavoured liqueur, although it can also be a clear, raspberry-flavoured brandy or a Belgian raspberry fruit beer.

❖ **Grenadine** is not actually a liqueur, as it is non-alcoholic, but it is a red, pomegranate-flavoured syrup used to colour and sweeten cocktails. A green version is also available.

Lapponia Lakka is a Finnish liqueur made from cloudberries. Cloudberries are closely related to the raspberry and grow in the cold northern climates of Scandinavia, Siberia, and Canada, as well as the Arctic Circle; they are one of the most delicious and costly of all berries because of their limited growing area. Because they grow in cold temperatures the berries ripen slowly, allowing the flavour to develop to an extraordinary intensity and sweetness, tasting almost like honeyed apples.

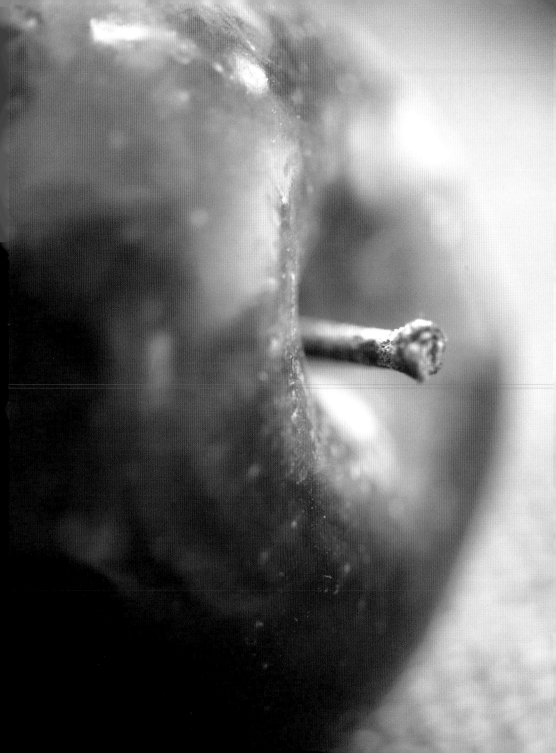

DRINKS MADE FROM APPLES AND PEARS

CIDER

To make cider, apples are pressed and the juice extracted from them is fermented. Most ciders are made from special cider apples, which are small, hard and inedible, but eating and cooking apples can also be used – the mix of fruit is an important factor in how a cider tastes. Once fermented, ciders are usually matured for several months to develop their full flavour.

Although it is also made in other places – for example Spain's Basque region, where it's called *sidra*, and in

Apples are tumbled through water to wash them thoroughly before pressing (left). Traditional cider presses were big wooden contraptions and had to be capable of producing sufficient force to crush the fruit to a pulp (above). The fruit was pressed by hand several times to make sure all the juice had been extracted. Modern plants use hydraulically operated plate presses.

CALVADOS

Calvados is a 40 per cent ABV fruit brandy made from fermented apple juice (cider) in Normandy and Brittany in northern France. The making of calvados is governed by *appellation contrôlée* rules and it must be aged for at least two years. Although commonly served both before and after eating, in France, during a rather long meal, a small glass of calvados is often drunk between courses to reinvigorate the appetite.

Northern France – cider is a traditional English drink and production tends to be associated with the West Country, but it is also made in counties such as Kent, Herefordshire and Worcestershire.

Cider can be dry or sweet, still or fizzy, dark and cloudy or light and clear. It can have an ABV of anything from 2 to about 8 per cent. It is made by both large commercial producers and smaller concerns, and is available on draught and in bottles. Rough, local cider is called scrumpy. The Campaign for Real Ale (CAMRA) also campaigns for real cider.

Mass-produced brands of cider include Magners, which was the first to introduce the concept of serving cider over ice, Merrydown and Strongbow.

In the United States, the word cider usually means non-alcoholic apple juice and the term for what's called cider in the UK is 'hard cider'.

While the French have cornered the market in calvados, cider brandy, which is basically the same thing, has been produced in England since the 17th century and the finest vintages are said to rival the French variety in colour, quality and taste.

APPLEJACK

Applejack is an American fruit brandy made from fermented apple juice (cider), with an ABV of around 40 per cent.

PERRY

This traditional English drink is similar to cider except that it is made from fermented pear, rather than apple, juice. The pears used are usually small, hard perry pears, rather than the dessert fruit, but not much perry is made and the drink is relatively hard to obtain, although the Campaign for Real Ale does campaign on its behalf.

BABYCHAM

Babycham is not, it has to be said, the most masculine of drinks, but it is a light sparkling perry with an ABV of 5.5 per cent. It goes in and out of fashion, but is enduringly associated with the 1970's advertising slogan 'I'll have a Babycham' and its jumping baby deer logo.

POIRE WILLIAM

Poire William is a pear liqueur made by steeping Bartlett pears in pear brandy.

PERA SEGNANA

Pera Segnana is a similar Italian liqueur.

These brandy stills, named Josephine and Fifi, were manufactured between the wars in Paris and are still used today to make cider brandy in England at Passvale Farm for the Somerset Cider Company.

65

DRINKS DERIVED FROM STARCH

Where to begin with beer? There are thousands of different beers and many different ways of making or brewing it, but essentially beer is fermented water and starch, although the exact constituents, including the minerals present in the water used, all affect the style, appearance and taste of the end product.

Beer can be made from wheat, rye, rice, potatoes, grasses such as sorghum or many other raw ingredients, but the most common source of starch

is malted barley. Malted means the grains have been encouraged to germinate and then dried before they actually grow. Malting helps develop the enzymes, or proteins that generate chemical reactions, which are needed to turn the starch into sugar, which can then be fermented.

Beer may be flavoured with a wide range of herbs and fruit, but the most common flavouring is hops, the flower of the hop vine. Hops impart a certain bitterness and also act as a preservative.

To cause fermentation, yeast is added, as this turns the sugar into alcohol and carbon dioxide. One particular type of yeast, known as brewer's yeast, has been used for centuries to make beer, but other types are also employed. Incidentally, brewer's yeast is a rich source of nutrients such as vitamin B, potassium and selenium, so although the effectiveness of many of these are reduced by the brewing process, there is some foundation for the claim that beer has health-giving properties.

Various types of clarifying agents, such as isinglass, a substance obtained from the swimbladders of fish, or carrageenan, derived from seaweed, can be added to get rid of the solid proteins in beer. In most beers, although not cask-conditioned ale and wheat beer, yeast sediment is also filtered out.

It is impossible to say who first brewed beer – it was probably invented by chance by various different societies at various different times – but 6,000 years ago the ancient Sumerians made it, and the Babylonians and Egyptians drank it too.

In the last 30 years or so there has been a revolution among discerning beer drinkers in the UK and the US, many of whom have rejected global brands in favour of local brews which have a more distinctive character. This has resulted in a thriving climate for smaller, regional brewers and 'microbreweries' that produce beers suited to local tastes.

In medieval Europe, monks did a lot of brewing, as drinking was permitted during a fast and beer was nutritious. Indeed, monks in what is now Belgium are believed to have been the first people to flavour beer with hops.

In modern times, the industrial revolution and scientific progress, such as the discovery of pasteurisation and the development of refrigeration, meant that beer could be brewed more efficiently, with greater control over the process and on a larger scale.

The temperature at which beer is best enjoyed depends on the type of beer and to an extent personal preference. However, standard bitter and stout are usually served at cellar temperature, and dark lager and wheat beer are usually lightly chilled, while pale lager tends to be chilled. See also ale, bitter, cask-conditioned ale, lager, lambic, pale ale, porter, stout and wheat beer.

ALE

Ale is beer brewed from barley malt and flavoured with hops. Types include bitter, brown ale, dark ale and pale ale. The descriptors loosely relate to the colour of the malt used, which is determined by how much and with what it is roasted. Ale is sometimes used as a general term to cover both beer and lager.

PALE ALE

Pale ale came about in the early 19th century, when new technologies enabled brewers to use lighter coloured malt to produce pale-golden coloured beer, known as pale ale. IPA (Indian Pale Ale), produced for export to the colonies, was slightly more alcoholic, at least 4 per cent ABV, and contained more hops,

MILD

Mild is a style of beer that was very popular in the UK in the first half of the 20th century, but which is now hard to find, as sales of bitter overtook it in the 1960s.

PORTER

Porter is a dark, bitter beer made from roasted, unmalted barley, which was very popular in the 18th century. Named for London's market workers, porter was generally quite strong, around 6 per cent ABV, but the porter revival of recent years, led by small British brewers and the microbreweries of the United States, has produced slightly less alcoholic porters with ABVs more likely to be around 4 per cent.

STOUT

Stout is a type of porter and Guinness is indisputably the most famous brand of stout available. Guinness was first brewed in Dublin in the mid-18th century by Arthur Guinness. The way the barley is roasted gives Guinness its distinctive colour and taste. It has relatively low levels of carbon dioxide, so it is not particularly fizzy, but it does contain nitrogen and it is the nitrogen bubbles that give it the characteristic creamy head. It is popular around the globe and especially in Ireland. A number of variants and strengths are available.

DRAUGHT GUINNESS

Draught Guinness should be served chilled, but because of the way it foams, the glass should initially be filled three-quarters of the way up to the rim. Once it has settled, the pint should be topped up. Bartenders with a whimsical bent sometimes draw a simple picture, perhaps a shamrock, in the head. Guinness is also sold in cans, which contain a special widget that

which helped keep the beer in good condition on long sea journeys. The popularity of bitter has since superseded that of pale ale, although IPA still survives as a relatively common epithet.

BITTER

Bitter is a style of beer that arose in the UK in the late 19th century, as brewers started to develop beers that could be made and sold quite quickly. It grew out of pale ale, but had a deeper bronze colour due to the use of slightly darker malt.

Theoretically, bitter has an ABV of between 3.4 and 3.9 per cent, while best bitter is stronger and has an ABV of 4 per cent upwards. However, the names of commercial products can sometimes be misleading. 'Extra' or 'special strong' bitter should have an ABV of 5 per cent upwards. The terms beer and bitter are often used interchangeably.

unleashes a stream of bubbles into the beer when the can is opened. Murphy's is another brand of dry stout, while Mackeson is an example of a sweet stout.

CASK-CONDITIONED ALE

Cask-conditioned ale is unfiltered and unpasteurised beer – or what the Campaign for Real Ale calls 'real ale'. The yeast is left in the barrel, so fermentation continues, giving the beer a fresh, just-brewed taste.

BARLEY WINE

Barley wine is actually a beer, which is dark and fruity, with a high alcohol content.

LAGER

One of the principal differences between beer and lager is that beer is brewed at higher temperatures with top-fermenting yeast (the yeast rises to the top of the vessel in which the beer is being brewed), while lager is brewed at lower temperatures with bottom-fermenting yeast (it doesn't rise). In fact, the name lager comes from the German word *lagern*, meaning 'to store', because lager is stored or 'lagered' for at least a few weeks, certainly longer than most other modern beers, in order to complete the bottom-fermentation process.

The malt used in lager tends to be lighter, so, compared to beer, lager has a lighter colour and a crisper, less hoppy flavour. Lager also tends to be fizzier and has a lower alcohol content, although of course there are plenty of strong lagers available. It is generally served chilled.

Lager was first brewed in Germany, in Bavaria, in the 16th century and the style developed because brewers stopped making beer in the summer, when the heat made it unstable and likely to go off. Instead they stored their winter brews in caves and cellars,

often chilling them with blocks of ice. They discovered that in these colder temperatures the yeast sunk to the bottom and the beer – now lager – was more stable.

The Germans take their lager seriously and in 1516 introduced the world's first food law – the *Reinheitsgebot* or Purity Law. This governs the ingredients of beer and states that beer can only be produced from barley, hops and water. Of course, the addition of yeast is now permitted, but otherwise the law remains the same and German brewers are obliged to adhere to it. This is why German beers and lagers are generally so clear and of such high quality.

PILSNER

Pilsner is a style of lager that was developed in Pilsen, in what is now the Czech Republic, in the mid-19th century. The town's brewers hired a Bavarian lager expert called Josef Groll to improve their product. He inducted them into the secrets of German brewing, but the use of local ingredients, in particular the local soft water, and light barley, gave rise to a light, clear, relatively fizzy drink, which subsequently became known as pilsner. Most modern pale lagers are based on the pilsner style.

Bock

Broadly speaking, bock is a heavier, darker (contrasted with pale) style of German lager, originally brewed in the northern German town of Einbeck, but now made in many variants across Germany, Austria and Holland.

Ice beer

Not to be confused with the recent trend for Extra Cold beers, ice beer is not colder than normal lager – but it is slightly stronger. The brew is chilled so that the water in it starts to freeze, but not the alcohol. Ice crystals are then skimmed off, resulting in less water and therefore greater strength. This method is how some of the world's strongest beers are made, such as the traditional German *Eisbock* EKU, which has an ABV of 13.5 per cent.

In the past ten years the global consumption of beer, and in particular bottled lager, has increased dramatically. In 2004 over 33 million gallons were consumed worldwide with drinkers in China, the USA and Germany leading the way. The biggest beer producer in the world is the American company Anheuser-Busch, which produces Budweiser among many brands, but the most widely available beer is Heineken.

Steam beer

This gets its name from the high level of carbonation in the beer which causes a hissing noise when casks are opened. This effervescence is due to using the lager method, with yeast at the bottom, with the higher temperatures used in ale brewing.

BEER AND LAGER BRANDS

❖ **Adnams** is a Suffolk-based brewer, which produces a bitter, the higher ABV Explorer and a range of seasonal beers, including Old Ale and Oyster Stout.

❖ **Asahi** is a Japanese brand of lager, which is well-known for Asahi Super Dry, which was one of the first of the less heavy lagers to be produced in Japan.

❖ **Beck's** is a German brand of lager. Its Bremen-based parent company is a major exporter and makes dark and citrus-flavoured products too.

❖ **Belhaven** is a brewer based just outside Edinburgh, which produces a range of beers, including St Andrews Ale and Belhaven 80 Shilling (the strength of Scottish beers used to be measured as 70, 80 or 90 shillings).

❖ **Boddingtons** bitter was originally brewed at the Strangeways Brewery in Manchester, but is now made in several locations and sold around the world.

❖ **Brahma** is a Brazilian brand of lager.

❖ **Brains** is a Cardiff-based brewer, which produces a range of beers, including Bread of Heaven and seasonal beers such as Land of My Fathers and St David's Ale.

❖ **Budweiser** is an American brand of lager, owned by the Anheuser-Busch company. Bud, as it is colloquially known, and Bud Light, which has a lower ABV and calorie-count, are among the top-selling lagers in the world.

❖ **Budweiser Budvar** is a Czech lager, brewed locally in the UK, but not to be confused with the well-known North American lager Budweiser – the right to the name Budweiser has been the subject of legal action in several countries.

❖ **Carling** is a lager, formerly known as Carling Black Label and famous for the slogan 'I bet he drinks Carling Black Label'.

❖ **Carlsberg's** parent company is headquartered in Copenhagen, Denmark, although the lager is brewed at various sites around the world. The same company also makes Special Brew, a strong canned lager with an ABV of 9 per cent.

❖ **Cobra** is a brand of Indian lager, brewed locally in the UK.

❖ **Coors** is a North American brand of lager, with many sub-brands.

❖ **Corona** is a Mexican brand of lager, often served with a wedge of lemon or lime inserted into the neck of the bottle, although this isn't usually done in Mexico.

❖ **Dos Equis** is a brand of Mexican lager.

❖ **Efes** is a Turkish brand of pilsner-style lager.

❖ **Fosters** is an Australian brand of lager, although it's brewed locally in the UK and other countries, and apparently isn't the top-selling lager in Australia itself.

❖ **Freedom** is a brand of organic micro-brewed lager and pilsner.

❖ **Fuller's** is a west London-based brewer that produces a range of beers, including London Pride and seasonal beers such as Jack Frost and London Porter.

❖ **Greene King** is a Suffolk-based brewer that produces Greene King IPA and owns sub-brands that include Abbot Ale, Old Speckled Hen and Ruddles County.

❖ **Grolsch** is a Dutch brand of lager, which is bottled with a distinctive swing-top cap and has a range of sub-brands.

❖ **Heineken** is a Dutch brand of lager, brewed at various sites around the world and with a range of sub-brands.

❖ **Kaliber** is a well-known alcohol-free lager that's made as a full-strength lager, but at the end of the brewing process the alcohol is all removed.

❖ **Kingfisher** is an Indian brand of lager.

❖ **Kronenbourg 1664** is a French brand of lager.

❖ **Marstons** is a Burton Upon Trent-based brewer that produces a range of beers, including Burton Bitter and Pedigree.

❖ **McEwans** is an Edinburgh-based brand of beer and lager, part of Scottish Newcastle plc.

❖ **Michelob** is an American brand of lager with a range of sub-brands.

❖ **Miller** is a brand of American lager. Its parent company has a range of sub-brands, including the low-alcohol Miller Lite.

❖ **Moretti** is an Italian lager, not dissimilar in style to German bock.

❖ **Newcastle Brown Ale** is a brand of dark, mild bottled beer.

❖ **Peroni** is an Italian brand of lager, its most famous product being Nastro Azzurro.

❖ **Pilsner Urquell** is a brand of Czech lager.

❖ **Red Stripe** is a Jamaican brand of lager, brewed locally in the UK.

❖ **Rolling Rock** is an American brand of lager. Some believe the 33 on the label relates to the repeal of prohibition in the United States in 1933, but it's more likely to be a reference to the drink's original slogan, which was 33 (rather long-winded) words long. A printer allegedly incorporated the number into the slogan by mistake.

❖ **Sagres** is a Portuguese brand of lager, brewed in the south of the country.

❖ **Sam Smith** is a Yorkshire-based brewer that produces a range of beers, including Old Brewery Bitter.

❖ **Sapporo** is a Japanese brand of lager brewed since 1877, initially by a brewmaster who had studied the art of beer-making in Germany. It is now brewed all over the world.

❖ **San Miguel** is a brand of Spanish lager.

❖ **Sol** is a brand of Mexican lager.

❖ **Staropramen** is a strong Czech lager.

❖ **Steinlager** is a New Zealand lager.

❖ **Stella Artois** is a Belgian lager, brewed at various sites around the world.

❖ **Super Bock** is a Portuguese brand of lager, brewed in the north of the country.

❖ **Tennent's** is a Scottish lager, with 9 per cent ABV.

❖ **Tetley** is a brand of beer, not to be confused with the tea of the same name.

❖ **Theakston** is a North Yorkshire-based brewer that produces a range of beers, including the fairly strong Old Peculier and seasonal beers such as Hogshead Bitter.

❖ **Tiger** is a brand of South-east Asian lager, brewed at various sites throughout the region.

❖ **Wychwood** is an Oxfordshire-based brewer, which produces a range of beers, including Legendary Hobgoblin and seasonal beers such as BeeWyched, brewed with Fairtrade honey.

❖ **Young's** is a south London-based brewer, which produces a range of beers, including Young's Bitter, Waggledance and Wells Bombardier.

❖ **Zima** is an alcopop or, according to its producer, malt beverage that's not dissimilar to a lager and is available in three citrus flavours. It's popular in the United States.

BELGIAN BEER

Belgium has a rich and varied brewing tradition. For example, it makes well-respected and somewhat unusual wheat beer, red beer, brown ale, Trappist and lambic beer, the latter being particularly prized by connoisseurs. How Belgian beer is served and drunk is heavily ritualised, and many brewers produce their own branded glasses, in shapes supposedly suitable for their type of brew. Belgian beer tends to be considerably stronger than the beer commonly drunk in the UK. It is not unusual to find ABVs of 10 and 11 per cent.

Unsurprisingly, wheat beer has a lot of wheat in it, although many wheat beers also contain malted barley. The style is generally associated with Belgium, where it's called *witbieren*, and Germany, where it's called *weissbier*. Both names actually mean white beer. This is a reference to their light colour, which comes from the yeast sediment. Wheat beers are sometimes a little sweet and sometimes a little fruity. They are also fairly light on the palate and have an ABV of around 5 per cent. Hoegaarden is a well-known brand of wheat beer.

To qualify as Trappist a beer must be brewed by Trappist monks, or at least made under their direct supervision. There are six Trappist breweries in Belgium. These are Achel, Chimay, Orval, Rochefort, Westmalle, Westvleteren and La Trappe. (There's also a Trappist brewery in Holland, called La Trappe.) The monks originally made beer for their own consumption, as a source of nourishment, especially during fasts and because the water wasn't safe to drink, but now the production of beer gives the abbeys an income.

Brewed only in Belgium, in an area called Paylottenland, south-west of Brussels, rather than being fermented with brewer's yeast, lambic is a style of beer that's produced by a process called spontaneous fermentation, in which the beer is exposed to airborne wild yeasts. This gives it a sour, almost cider-like flavour.

DRINKS DISTILLED FROM SUGAR

RUM

Today rum is made all over the world, but it is most strongly associated with the Caribbean, where it was first made in the 17th century by slaves who worked on the sugarcane plantations.

Rum is made by fermenting and then distilling molasses, the thick, syrupy by-product of sugarcane processing, that is called treacle in the UK. The resulting liquid is clear and is usually described as

light, white or silver rum, but this is often aged in oak barrels or coloured with caramel to make dark, amber, golden or black rum.

There isn't a single standard for rum production, individual countries have their own, and similar styles of rum can have different names, even within the Caribbean. For this reason it's hard to give a firm ABV for rum, but it's generally around 40 per cent, although if a rum is described as overproof it could have an ABV of approaching double that.

Rum can be turned into a liqueur and spiced or flavoured with citrus fruit, mango or coconut. It is the basis for a number of well-known cocktails, for instance a Cuba Libre, a Mai Tai, a Daiquiri and, of course, a Rum Punch – or it can be mixed with, say, cola, but it can also be drunk straight, either with or without ice.

RUM BRANDS

❖ **Appleton Estate** is a brand of aged Jamaican rum.
❖ **Bacardi** is a brand of white rum. The Bacardi company was originally founded in Cuba in the late 19th century, but the family that owns it left there after the Cuban Revolution in 1959 and the business is now based in Bermuda, although it has offshoots all over the Caribbean and indeed the world. As well as various rums, Bacardi makes the Bacardi Breezer range of alcopop pre-mixed rum and fruit drinks that are popular with young people.

- **Malibu** is not a pure rum. It is a white rum-based liqueur with a strong coconut taste, although versions with additional fruit flavourings are also available. Made in Barbados, it has an ABV of 21 per cent and can be served neat, with ice or mixed with a soft drink. Its distinctive logo shows crossed palm trees and a setting sun.
- **Mount Gay** is a brand of Barbadian rum, first produced in 1703 and available in several styles and flavours.
- **Wray and Nephews** is a brand of Jamaican rum – Wray and Nephews White Overproof rum has a rather high ABV of 63 per cent.
- **Wood's Old Navy** is a brand of Guyanan rum. Its makers claim it has the highest ABV – 57 per cent – of any rum on the market.

CACHAÇA

This sugar cane spirit or rum is the national drink of Brazil, being the most popular distilled alcoholic beverage in that country, and it is an essential ingredient in the classic cocktail Caipirinha. White cachaca is unaged, while dark cachaça, seen as the premium version, is aged in wooden barrels.

- **Barbancourt** is a brand of Haitian rum or rhum, as it says on the label, that is made from sugar cane juice, rather than molasses, and, like cognac, is double-distilled.
- **Captain Morgan** is a brand of dark rum, apparently named after a Welsh pirate called Sir Henry Morgan.
- **Havana Club** is a brand of Cuban rum. Founded in the late 19th century, Havana Club was nationalised after the Cuban Revolution of 1959 and its various rums, including some prized aged ones, are sold around the world by the Cuban Government, in a joint venture with the makers of Pernod and Ricard.

CHOCOLATE LIQUEUR BRANDS

- **Ashanti Gold** is a Danish chocolate liqueur.
- **Creme de cacao** is a syrupy chocolate liqueur flavoured with cocoa and vanilla beans that has an ABV of between 25 and 30 per cent. It is usually clear, but dark crème de cacao is caramel-coloured.
- **Godiva** is a chocolate liqueur with an ABV of 17 per cent, which comes in dark, milk, white and mocha flavours.
- **Mozart** is a milk chocolate liqueur, also available in dark and white chocolate versions.

To get the alcohol into a liqueur chocolate, boiling sugar syrup is poured on to the alcohol. The mixture is cooled for more than 15 hours. In cooling, the sugar forms a chrysalis around the alcohol. After they are completely cooled, the capsules are carefully taken from the moulds, brushed and covered in melted dark chocolate. The manufacturing process of these chocolates takes more than two days.

NON-ALCOHOLIC FLAVOURINGS MADE WITH SUGAR

❖ **Cordial** is a sweet, fruit-flavoured syrup that is diluted to taste, for example elderflower cordial, or used in a cocktail. In the United States, cordial is sometimes used to mean liqueur.

❖ **Gomme syrup** is a non-alcoholic syrup made of sugar and water, and thickened with gum arabic, used to sweeten cocktails.

❖ **Orgeat syrup** is a non-alcoholic, almond-flavoured syrup used to sweeten cocktails.

❖ **Sour mix** is a mixture of sugar syrup and lemon juice, also known as sweet and sour mix or bar mix.

❖ **Sugar syrup** is used for sweetening drinks. This is liquid sugar and it can be either clear or brown. It can be bought commercially or home-made by dissolving two parts sugar in one part water (see recipe on page 15). Sugar syrup can also be called simple syrup, simple sugar syrup or bar syrup.

DRINKS DISTILLED FROM AGAVE

MEZCAL

This is a distilled spirit made from a succulent (not a cactus, by the way) called agave, produced throughout Mexico, but particularly around Oaxaca. Foreign bodies are often added to bottles of mezcal (mescal), the most famous being a 'worm', although this isn't really a worm, it is either a weevil or the larva of a moth.

TEQUILA

A mezcal produced exclusively in the Jarisco region of Mexico. Only tequila is made from the roasted heart of the blue agave, one of the 136 species of agave that grow in Mexico and a plant that takes around a decade to mature.

The forerunner of tequila was called pulque, a beer-like fermented agave drink made by the indigenous Mexicans, but when the Spanish Conquistadors arrived in the 16th century they soon developed a stronger tipple by distilling agave syrup. Tequila is usually distilled twice, which gives it an ABV of around 40 per cent.

Tequila is drunk neat, often from a special narrow glass called a *caballito*, but in Mexico it is not, apparently, downed in one with a lick of salt and a suck of lime as a tequila slammer. Contrary to popular belief, you never get a 'worm' in the bottom of a bottle of tequila either.

Tequila has five classifications. The original, and most common, is *blanco* (white) or *plata* (silver), which is unaged and consequently can be quite harsh, although it may have more agave flavour than other types. The second type is *oro* (gold) tequila, which is essentially *blanco* with colouring and flavouring added, to make it look older and taste smoother. Next is *reposado* (rested), which is aged for up to a year in wooden casks. This darkens the colour and the tequila takes on flavouring from the wood. *Anejo* (vintage) is aged from one to ten years, generally making it even darker and more woody. Finally, there is *extra anejo* (ultra aged), which is kept in cask for a minimum of three years and, again, up to ten.

However, there are also two categories of tequila – 100 per cent agave or *puro de agave*, which is what the connoisseurs usually prefer, and simple tequila, which is also known as *mixto*. This contains just over 50 per cent agave, the rest being other fermented sugars. If the label doesn't say 100 per cent agave, it isn't. Well-known brands of tequila include Cuervo and Sauza.

SOTOL

Sotol is a distilled spirit similar to mezcal, made in the Chihuahua area of Mexico from a plant called the desert spoon, but rarely exported.

DRINKS DISTILLED FROM RICE

SAKE

Although it is commonly described as Japanese rice wine, sake is much more like rice beer, due to the way in which it is fermented, which is much closer to

the process used for beer. The first sake was probably made by people chewing and then spitting out rice, so that their saliva could activate natural fermentation. However, at some point in history a mould was discovered that meant the mastication stage could be bypassed, and today sake production is appropriately high-tech.

Sake is generally filtered, so it is clear, but needless to say there are lots of different types of sake, some not even made from rice. It tends to be served neat. Sake is unusual in that it is an alcoholic drink that can be consumed cold, warm or hot, depending on the season, the quality of the sake and the drinker's own preference. It is traditionally poured from a flask into a shallow cup, and there are many Japanese rituals associated with it. For instance, drinking from someone else's cup apparently signals friendship.

SHOCHU

Shochu is a clear Japanese spirit distilled from rice or sweet potato wine. It is similar to vodka.

SOJU

Soju is a clear spirit from Korea, distilled from fermented rice, but not dissimilar in taste to a slightly sweet vodka, with an ABV of between 20 and 45 per cent.

DRINKS MADE FROM BEANS AND LEAVES

COFFEE

To make coffee, the roasted and ground beans of the coffee plant are steeped in hot water. There are a range of methods for doing this, including filtering, percolating or using an espresso machine, and a whole culture and set of rituals surround this process. Coffee is often used to flavour liqueurs, and hot coffee mixed with Irish whiskey and sugar, and topped with whipped cream, makes the after-dinner drink Irish coffee.

Well-known coffee liqueurs include Kahlúa, a Mexican 25 per cent ABV, and Tia Maria, a rum-based Jamaican 26.5 per cent ABV coffee liqueur flavoured with the best Jamaican blue mountain coffee beans.

Coffee contains caffeine, as do most colas and Red Bull, a brand of non-alcoholic, fizzy energy drink. Along with the caffeine, Red Bull also has an amino acid derivative called taurine in it. It's drunk to combat physical and mental exhaustion, but is also commonly mixed with spirits.

TEA

This is a drink made from the dried leaves of the tea bush, infused in hot water. Milk and sometimes sugar are generally added to the hot beverage, but it can also be cooled and drunk black, sweetened with sugar syrup and served with a slice of lemon. This is known as iced tea. Cold, weak tea is also one of the ingredients in a Long Island tea cocktail.

TYPES OF WATER

MINERAL WATER

Essentially mineral water is water containing minerals, such as salts. Those minerals may be present in natural still spring water or they can be added when the water is bottled, although most countries have regulations governing the production of mineral water. Likewise, mineral water may be naturally carbonated or carbon dioxide can be added. Carbonated mineral water is also known as sparkling water or fizzy water. Soda water is very similar, but is more likely to have added salts, particularly sodium bicarbonate, as are the American variants club soda and selzer water.

British brands of mineral water include Buxton, Hildon and Highland Spring, all of which come in still and sparkling varieties. French brands include Evian and Volvic, which are both still, and Perrier, which is sparkling. San Pellegrino is an Italian brand of sparkling mineral water.

TONIC WATER

This carbonated water contains quinine, which was originally added to protect against malaria, rife in the drink's initial target markets of Africa and India (the product is sometimes known as Indian tonic water). However, modern versions only contain tiny amounts of quinine. This gives the drink a slightly bitter taste, but makes it mix well with gin and vodka. Canada Dry and Schweppes are well-known brands of tonic water.

WAKE-UP CALL

Although it is not to be recommended, a cocktail can be just the way to start the day, particularly at the weekend when you have got a lazy day ahead. Fruity, fizzy, creamy or caffeine-based, any of the recipes featured here will make a perfect accompaniment to that late breakfast or leisurely brunch.

BANANA DAIQUIRI ◂

Rum and lime juice are the base of a classic Daiquiri. Here the addition of bananas and cream make for a rich and fortifying version.

SERVES 1
2 measures white rum
½ measure triple sec
½ measure lime juice
½ measure single cream
1 tsp sugar syrup
¼ banana, peeled and sliced
lime wedge

In a blender, process the white rum, triple sec, lime juice, cream, sugar syrup and banana until smooth. Then pour the mixture, without straining, into a chilled cocktail glass or lowball glass and dress with a wedge of lime.

Famously a favourite of American writer Ernest Hemingway and President John F. Kennedy, the Daiquiri is named after a small town in Cuba and was allegedly invented at the turn of the 20th century by an American engineer, who was working there, ran out of gin and turned to rum. However, given the prevalence of rum in Cuba it is probable that the locals had discovered this delicious drink some time previously.

Rum, lime juice and a little sugar or syrup are the base of a classic Daiquiri, but you can blend it with ice to make a frozen Daiquiri or add just about any fruit.

Whatever else goes into a Daiquiri, though, it is important to squeeze the lime by hand so that the oils from the peel mix with the juice and impart a sharp, intense flavour to the cocktail.

MAIDEN'S PRAYER

This is similar to a Chelsea Sidecar (page 168), but the orange juice in a Maiden's Prayer will give you an extra little sugar boost too.

SERVES 1
1 measure gin
1 measure triple sec
1 tsp orange juice
1 tsp lemon juice
twist of lemon peel

Pour the gin, triple sec, orange juice and lemon juice over ice cubes, shake vigorously until well frosted, and strain into a chilled cocktail glass. Garnish with a twist of lemon peel.

It's not clear quite why the bride's mother should favour this tipple, but the combination of both sloe gin and gin gives it a delicious flavour and some potency.

BRIDE'S MOTHER ▸

SERVES 1
1½ measures sloe gin
1 measure gin
2½ measures grapefruit juice
½ measure sugar syrup
lemon slice

Pour the sloe gin, gin, grapefruit juice and sugar syrup over ice cubes, shake vigorously until well frosted, and strain into a chilled cocktail glass with a slice of lemon.

SEVENTH HEAVEN ‹

SERVES 1
2 measures gin
½ measure maraschino
½ measure grapefruit juice
fresh mint sprig

*Pour the gin, maraschino and grapefruit juice over ice
cubes and shake vigorously until well frosted. Strain into
a chilled cocktail glass and dress with fresh mint.*

MELON BALL ‹

SERVES 1
2 measures vodka
2 measures Midori
4 measures pineapple juice
cracked ice
melon wedge

*Pour the vodka, Midori and pineapple juice over ice
cubes and stir well to mix. Half fill a chilled highball glass
with cracked ice and strain the cocktail over it. Decorate
with a wedge of melon.*

MELON STATE BALL ▾

SERVES 1
2 measures vodka
1 measure Midori
2 measures orange juice

Pour the vodka, Midori and orange juice over ice cubes and shake vigorously until well frosted. Strain into a chilled cocktail glass.

GENOA VODKA ▴

SERVES 1
2 measures vodka
1 measure Campari
3 measures orange juice
orange slice

Pour the vodka, Campari and orange juice over ice cubes and shake vigorously until well frosted. Strain into a small chilled lowball glass and dress with a slice of orange.

LAST MANGO IN PARIS ◄

SERVES 1
2 measures vodka
1 measure framboise
1 measure lime juice
½ mango, peeled, stoned and chopped
2 strawberries, halved
lime slice
1 strawberry

Whizz the vodka, framboise, lime juice, mango and halved strawberries in a blender until slushy. Pour into a chilled cocktail glass or sour glass and dress with a slice of lime and the extra strawberry.

BLUE MONDAY

The lovely colour and fruity flavour of this cocktail is guaranteed to make Monday your favourite day of the week.

SERVES 1
cracked ice
1 measure vodka
½ measure Cointreau
1 tbsp blue curaçao

Put the cracked ice into a mixing glass or jug and pour in the vodka, Cointreau and curaçao. Stir well and strain into a cocktail glass.

LADY

SERVES 1
2 measures gin
1 measure peach brandy
1 measure lemon juice
1 tsp egg white

Shake the gin, peach brandy and lemon juice over ice cubes with the egg white until well frosted. Strain into a chilled cocktail glass.

BEAGLE

SERVES 1
cracked ice
dash of kümmel
dash of lemon juice
2 measures brandy
1 measure cranberry juice

Put the cracked ice into a mixing glass. Add the dash of kümmel and the dash of lemon juice, then pour in the brandy and cranberry juice. Stir well to mix and strain into a chilled cocktail glass.

WALK TALL

This looks and smells like orange juice, but don't be deceived, there's lots going on here.

SERVES 1
½ measure sweet white vermouth
¼ measure gin
¼ measure Campari
¼ measure orange liqueur
sweet orange juice
soda water
orange peel

Thoroughly mix the vermouth, gin, Campari, orange liqueur and orange juice and pour into a highball glass full of ice cubes. Top up with a splash of soda water if you wish and decorate with a twist of orange peel.

BACHELOR'S BAIT

SERVES 1
2 measures gin
1 tsp grenadine
1 egg white
dash of orange bitters

Shake the gin, grenadine and egg white together over ice cubes until well frosted. Add a dash of orange bitters, give the mixture another quick shake and strain into a chilled cocktail glass.

STRAWBERRY COLADA ◄

SERVES 1

4–6 ice cubes, crushed

3 measures golden rum

4 measures pineapple juice

1 measure coconut cream

6 strawberries, hulled

pineapple wedge

extra strawberry

In a blender, whizz together the crushed ice, rum, pineapple juice, coconut cream and hulled strawberries. Blend until smooth, then pour, without straining, into a chilled highball glass. Dress with a wedge of pineapple and a strawberry.

This version of a Piña Colada, which literally means 'strained pineapple', is made extra fruity – and somewhat pinky – by the delicious addition of strawberries.

ESPRESSO GALLIANO ▲

This variant on an Irish Coffee is an excellent way to start the day, but it tastes best without the traditional cream.

SERVES 1

2 measures Galliano

freshly made strong black coffee

sugar to taste

lemon or orange juice

twist of orange peel

Put the Galliano into a warmed heatproof glass. Pour in the coffee, add a teaspoon or two of sugar and a splash of lemon or orange juice to taste and stir. Serve with a twist of orange peel.

WEDDING BELLE ▶

This would set you up nicely for the big day.

SERVES 1
2 measures gin
2 measures Dubonnet
1 measure cherry brandy
1 measure orange juice
twist of orange peel

Shake the gin, Dubonnet, cherry brandy and orange juice over ice cubes until well frosted. Strain into a cocktail glass and serve with a twist of orange peel.

BLOODY MARY

SERVES 1
cracked ice
2 measures vodka
4 measures tomato juice
½ measure lemon juice
2 dashes of Worcestershire sauce
dash of Tabasco sauce
celery salt
black pepper
lemon wedge
celery stick

Pour the vodka, tomato juice, lemon juice, Worcestershire sauce and Tabasco over cracked ice, shake vigorously and season with the celery salt and black pepper. Strain into an iced old-fashioned glass and dress with the wedge of lemon and stick of celery.

IS THIS ALL? ▶

Suffice to say that this citrus combination is more than enough to fill your morning with optimism.

SERVES 1
2 measures lemon vodka
1 measure triple sec
1 measure lemon juice
1 egg white

Shake the lemon vodka, triple sec, lemon juice and egg white over ice cubes until well frosted. Strain into a chilled cocktail glass.

FUZZY MARTINI

SERVES 1

2 measures vanilla vodka

½ measure coffee vodka

1 tsp peach schnapps

peach slice

Shake the vanilla vodka, coffee vodka and peach schnapps over ice cubes until well frosted. Strain into a chilled cocktail glass and dress with a slice of peach.

GOLDEN FLIP

Sherry and almond liqueur are the bases for this flip, with an added kick of vodka.

SERVES 1

1 measure vodka

1 measure sweet sherry

1 measure amaretto

1 egg yolk

1 tbsp caster sugar

grated nutmeg

Pour all the ingredients except the nutmeg over ice cubes and shake well until frosted. Strain into a chilled wine glass and sprinkle with freshly grated nutmeg.

THIS IS IT

Is it? See what you think.

SERVES 1
cracked ice
2 measures gin
1 measure triple sec
1 measure lemon juice
1 egg white

Pour the gin, triple sec, lemon juice and egg white over cracked ice, shake vigorously until well frosted, then strain the mixture into a chilled cocktail glass.

POLYNESIA

SERVES 1
cracked ice
2 measures white rum
2 measures passion fruit juice
1 measure lime juice
1 egg white
dash of Angostura bitters

Pour the rum, passion fruit juice, lime juice and egg white over cracked ice with a dash of Angostura bitters and shake until well frosted. Strain into a chilled cocktail glass.

APPLE BLOSSOM ◀

SERVES 1
2 measures brandy
1½ measures apple juice
½ tsp lemon juice
lemon slice

Pour the brandy, apple juice and lemon juice over ice cubes in a mixing glass and stir well. Half fill a chilled lowball glass with ice cubes and strain the cocktail over them. Dress with the slice of lemon.

PASSIONATE DAIQUIRI ◄

This twist on the traditional Daiquiri introduces the delicate flavour of passion fruit to the rum and lime.

SERVES 1

2 measures white rum

1 measure lime juice

½ measure passion fruit syrup

1 cocktail cherry

Pour the rum, lime juice and passion fruit syrup over ice cubes and shake vigorously until well frosted. Strain into a chilled cocktail glass and decorate with a cocktail cherry.

CREAMY SCREWDRIVER ▲

By adding a protein-rich egg yolk to the classic Screwdriver (page 296) you'll be set up for the day.

SERVES 1

2 measures vodka

crushed ice

6 measures orange juice

1 egg yolk

½ tsp sugar syrup

cracked ice

orange slice

In a blender mix the vodka, crushed ice, orange juice, egg yolk and sugar syrup until smooth. Half fill a chilled highball glass with cracked ice and pour the cocktail over them without straining. Serve with a slice of orange.

TITANIC ▾

A genuine iceberg adds authenticity but, if you can't get it, ordinary cracked ice works perfectly well too.

SERVES 1
3 measures mandarin liqueur
2 measures vodka
cracked ice
sparkling water

Pour the mandarin liqueur and vodka over ice cubes and shake vigorously until well frosted. Half fill a chilled highball glass or lowball glass with cracked ice and strain the cocktail over it. Top up with sparkling water.

SLOW COMFORTABLE SCREW

SERVES 1
2 measures sloe gin
orange juice
cracked ice
orange slice

Shake the sloe gin and orange juice with the cracked ice until well frosted and pour into a chilled highball glass. Decorate with a slice of orange.

The simple, classic 'Screw' has given rise to numerous and increasingly elaborate variations. However, you should always use freshly squeezed orange juice to make this refreshing cocktail – it's just not the same with bottled juice.

MEXICOLA

SERVES 1
cracked ice
2 measures tequila
1 measure lime juice
cola
lime or lemon slice

Half fill a chilled highball glass with the cracked ice.
Pour the tequila and lime juice over the ice and top
up with cola. Stir gently and decorate with a slice
of lime or lemon.

BOURBON MILK PUNCH

SERVES 1
2 measures bourbon
3 measures milk
1 tsp clear honey
dash of vanilla essence
freshly grated nutmeg

Shake the bourbon, milk, honey and vanilla essence
over ice cubes until well frosted. Strain into a chilled
highball glass or lowball glass and sprinkle with
freshly grated nutmeg.

LEMON SHERBET ▶

This turns into a delicious fluffy thick drink that you may well need a spoon for.

SERVES 1

2 measures gin

1 measure lemon juice

1 measure cream

½ measure orange curaçao

1 tsp caster sugar

dash of orange flower water

a little crushed ice

Whizz all the ingredients together in a blender for 10-15 seconds. Pour into a chilled lowball glass or highball glass and serve with straws.

DIAMOND FIZZ

SERVES 1

2 measures gin

½ measure lemon juice

1 tsp sugar syrup

champagne, chilled

Shake the gin, lemon juice and sugar syrup over ice cubes until well frosted. Strain into a chilled flute and top up with chilled champagne.

KIRSCH RICKEY ▶

The main characteristic of a Rickey is that it is refreshingly sharp, but here the kirsch and fresh cherries add just a tiny hint of sweetness.

SERVES 1

crushed ice

2 measures kirsch

1 tbsp lime juice

sparkling water

a few fresh cherries or olives, stoned

Pour the kirsch and lime juice into a chilled lowball glass half-filled with crushed ice. Top up with sparkling water and stir gently. Decorate with stoned fresh cherries or olives.

MISSISSIPPI MULE ◄

The Mississippi Mule has no ingredients in common
with its famous cousin the Moscow Mule (page 156),
but it delivers quite a kick nonetheless.

SERVES 1
2 measures gin
½ measure crème de cassis
½ measure lemon juice

*Pour the gin, crème de cassis and lemon juice over ice
cubes, shake vigorously until well frosted, and strain
into a small chilled lowball glass.*

HARLEM ▲

SERVES 1
2 measures gin
1½ measures pineapple juice
1 tsp maraschino
1 tbsp fresh pineapple, chopped
pineapple leaf

*Shake the gin, pineapple juice and maraschino over ice
cubes. Add the chopped fresh pineapple and shake
again until well frosted. Strain into a chilled lowball glass
and garnish with a pineapple leaf.*

ORANGE BLOSSOM

SERVES 1
cracked ice
2 measures gin
2 measures orange juice
orange slice

Pour the gin and orange juice over the cracked ice and shake vigorously until well frosted. Strain into a chilled cocktail glass and decorate with a slice of orange.

CHANGUIRONGO ▲

SERVES 1
cracked ice
2 measures white tequila
ginger ale
lime or lemon slice

Half fill a chilled highball glass with the cracked ice. Pour in the tequila and top up with the ginger ale. Stir gently and dress with a slice of lime or lemon.

During Prohibition in the USA, gin was often literally made in the bathtub and flavoured with fresh orange juice to conceal its filthy flavour. Made with good quality gin, which needs no such concealment, the Orange Blossom is delightfully refreshing.

DUKE ▲

A Buck's Fizz – simply orange juice and champagne – is a gently refreshing cocktail. The Duke is similar, but the addition of triple sec ups the orange flavour, the alcohol content and the vigour of the alarm call.

SERVES 1
1 measure triple sec
½ measure lemon juice
½ measure orange juice
1 egg white
dash of maraschino
champagne or sparkling wine, chilled

Pour the triple sec, lemon juice, orange juice, egg white and a dash of maraschino over ice cubes and shake vigorously until well frosted. Strain into a chilled wine glass and top up with chilled champagne or sparkling wine

AMERICAN MILLIONAIRE ▲

SERVES 1
1 measure rye whiskey
½ measure grenadine
½ measure curaçao
½ egg white
dash of Pernod

Shake the rye whiskey, grenadine, curaçao and egg white together over ice cubes. Strain into a wine glass and at the last minute add a dash of Pernod

CLOVER CLUB

SERVES 1
2 measures gin
1 measure lime juice
1 measure grenadine
1 egg white

Pour the gin, lime juice and grenadine over ice cubes. Add the egg white and shake vigorously until well frosted. Strain into a chilled cocktail glass.

WHY NOT? ▸

SERVES 1
cracked ice
dash of lemon juice
2 measures gin
1 measure peach brandy
1 measure Noilly Prat
twist of lemon peel

Put the cracked ice into a mixing glass and splash a dash of lemon juice over them. Pour in the gin, peach brandy and Noilly Prat, and stir to mix. Strain the liquid into a chilled cocktail glass. Serve with a twist of lemon peel.

PLANTER'S TEA ◂

Some people can't move until they've had a cuppa. This one should really get you going.

SERVES 1
2 measures strong black tea
2 measures dark rum
300 ml/10 fl oz orange juice
150 ml/5 fl oz fresh lemon juice
orange slices

Mix the tea, dark rum, orange juice and fresh lemon juice together. Heat gently, sweeten to taste and serve in an Irish Coffee glass or mug with slices of orange.

ACADEMIA DA CACHAÇA

RIO DE JANEIRO

This modest Rio bar was mixing Caipirinhas long before the Brazilian drink became a global standard. This classy yet casual place is a revelation to those who think of a Caipirinha as a simple mixture of lime, sugar, ice and the sugar-cane rum cachaça. Indeed, it transpires there are many sorts of cachaça and you'll simply never find a greater range anywhere else. After more than 22 years in business, the Academia's Caipirinhas are still widely acknowledged as the best in Brazil, and it also mixes the spirit into other award-winning cocktails.

Beneath an unusual Brazilian flag ceiling decoration made from raffia. the bar showcases a private connoisseur's collection of 2000

BEST FOR
Caipirinhas and cachaça

CAIPIRINHA ACADÊMICA

The signature Caipirinha Acadêmica is a cocktail of muddled citron, honey and the artisanal cachaça brand, Seleta. Both the cocktail and Seleta, which is produced in the Brazilian state of Minas Gerais, have become bestsellers at the Academia da Cachaça.

SERVES 1

2 citrons (similar in
appearance to a lemon,
with a highly fragrant peel)
125 g/4½ oz honey
3 measures Cachaça Seleta

Wash the citrons. Cut them into pieces and place them in a glass. Sprinkle with the honey and crush the citron pieces, pulp side up, with a pestle. (Academia da Cachaça has a long, wooden Brazilian one made specifically for this purpose.) Add the cachaça and stir to mix. Add ice cubes and stir again.

❖

'The key is to choose the right fruit, to squeeze, muddle or crush it to get the most flavour, and then to concentrate on getting the quantities of cachaça, ice and sugar just right.'

Barman, Antonio Marcos

cachaça bottles, arranged thematically to present the drink's 130-year history. The drinks list is scarcely less generous, with a hundred or so different regional cachaças alongside spiced and fruit-infused varieties. The oldest bottle dates back to 1875, while there are many artisanal brands, including Lua Cheia, a fruity golden liqueur. Passion fruit and coconut batida cocktails come with real fruit pieces and juice.

Partners Edméa Falcão, Renata Quinderé and Hélcio Santos wanted cachaça to be taken seriously, and that's an aim they've certainly achieved. But the Academia is also a much-lauded restaurant, serving north-east Brazilian specialities. As you sample shredded beef with cassava cream purée and sip your drink, you have to reflect there's nothing better than returning to the source. And so it is with Caipirinhas.

ACADEMIA DA CACHAÇA
Rua Conde Bernadotte 26
(Loja G)
Leblon
CEP 22430-200
Rio de Janeiro
Brazil
+ 55 21 2529 2680
www.academiadacachaca.com.br

Open daily
12.00 p.m. until the last customer leaves

LOUNGING AROUND

In this day and age none of us spends enough time in relaxation mode. However, when you do find time to sit by the pool, hang out with friends in the park, flick through a magazine on the sofa or snuffle through the afternoon movie, make sure you have one of these delicious cocktails beside you.

FROZEN MINT JULEP ‹

The precise origins of the Mint Julep are lost in the mists of time, but the cocktail was probably first made somewhere in the southern United States in the 18th century. This version is delicious.

SERVES 1
crushed ice
2 measures bourbon whiskey
1 measure lemon juice
1 measure sugar syrup
6 fresh mint leaves
fresh mint sprig

Put the crushed ice into a blender or food processor, add the bourbon, lemon juice, sugar syrup and fresh mint leaves, and blend at low speed until slushy. Pour into a chilled lowball glass and dress with a fresh mint sprig.

The word 'julep' probably derives from the Arabic word *julab*, meaning 'rosewater', and a julep has been a sweet, medicinal drink since at least the 15th century. Today, the Mint Julep cocktail is regarded as the quintessential drink of the southern United States.

Mint Juleps are traditionally served in a special silver or pewter julep cup, which is held only by the bottom or top edges, to allow the condensation to turn to frost. One would be particularly apt for this Frozen Mint Julep. However, if you don't have a suitable tankard to hand, a Collins glass, highball glass or tumbler will more than suffice. Use a good quality bourbon or whiskey, though, and fresh mint is absolutely essential.

STAR DAISY ▸

A Daisy is a cocktail with a high proportion of alcohol that is sweetened with fruit syrup. Perhaps it gets its name from the now old-fashioned slang, when the word 'daisy' referred to something exceptional and special.

SERVES 1

2 measures gin

1½ measures apple brandy

1½ measures lemon juice

1 tsp sugar syrup

½ tsp triple sec

soda water

Pour the gin, apple brandy, lemon juice, sugar syrup and triple sec over ice cubes and shake vigorously. Strain into a chilled lowball glass and top up with soda water.

GIN SLINGER ◂

SERVES 1

1 tsp sugar

1 measure lemon juice

1 tsp water

2 measures gin

twist of orange peel

Stir the sugar, lemon juice and water together until the sugar has dissolved. Pour in the gin and stir again. Half fill a chilled lowball glass with ice cubes and strain the cocktail over them. Decorate with a twist of orange peel.

BRANDY CUBAN ▸

SERVES 1
1½ measures brandy
½ measure lime juice
cola
lime slice

*Pour the brandy and lime juice into a lowball glass
half-filled with ice cubes. Top up with cola and stir gently.
Dress with a slice of lime.*

CRANBERRY COLLINS

The classic Collins drink is made with gin, but its
many variations are made with other spirits, so try this
one for size...

SERVES 1
2 measures vodka
¾ measure elderflower cordial
3 measures white cranberry and apple juice
soda water
lime slice

*Shake the vodka, elderflower cordial, and white cranberry
and apple juice over ice cubes until well frosted. Strain
into a highball glass with more ice cubes and top up
with soda to taste. Dress with a slice of lime.*

JAMAICA MULE ▸

SERVES 1

2 measures white rum
1 measure dark rum
1 measure golden rum
1 measure falernum
1 measure lime juice
ginger beer
pineapple wedges
crystallised ginger

Pour the white, dark and golden rums, falernum and lime juice over ice cubes and shake vigorously until well frosted. Strain the mixture into a chilled highball glass and top up with ginger beer. Dress the drink with wedges of pineapple and chunks of crystallised ginger.

BLINKER ▴

SERVES 1

2 measures rye whiskey
2½ measures grapefruit juice
1 tsp grenadine

Pour the rye whiskey, grapefruit juice and grenadine over ice cubes and shake vigorously until well frosted. Strain into a chilled cocktail glass.

Falernum, which features in the Jamaica Mule, is a sweet, slightly alcoholic, fairly thick syrup, flavoured with ginger, almonds and lime, and sometimes cloves, allspice or vanilla. It's often used in tropical or Caribbean drinks.

GIN SLING COCKTAIL ◄

SERVES 1

large chunk of ice
juice of ¾ lemon
½ tbsp icing sugar
1 measure gin
still water
lemon slice
dash of Angostura bitters

Put the large chunk of ice, lemon juice, icing sugar and gin into a lowball glass. Top up with still water. Float a slice of lemon on top and add a dash of Angostura bitters.

RUM DAISY ◄

SERVES 1

2 measures golden rum
1 measure lemon juice
1 tsp sugar syrup
½ tsp grenadine
cracked ice
orange slice

Pour the golden rum, lemon juice, sugar syrup, and grenadine over ice cubes and shake until well frosted. Half fill a chilled lowball glass with the cracked ice and strain the cocktail over it. Dress the drink with a slice of orange.

BANANA COLADA ‹

SERVES 1
4–6 ice cubes, crushed
2 measures white rum
4 measures pineapple juice
1 measure Malibu
1 banana, peeled and sliced
pineapple wedges

Whizz the crushed ice in a blender with the white rum, pineapple juice, Malibu and sliced banana. Blend until smooth, then pour, without straining, into a chilled highball glass and serve with pineapple wedges and a straw.

Long Island Iced Tea – originally a simple combination of vodka and a dash of cola – dates back to the days of American Prohibition, when it was drunk out of cups in an attempt to fool the FBI that it was innocuous iced tea.

LONG ISLAND ICED TEA

SERVES 1
2 measures vodka
1 measure gin
1 measure white tequila
1 measure white rum
½ measure white crème de menthe
2 measures lemon juice
1 tsp sugar syrup
cracked ice
cola
lime or lemon slice

Pour the vodka, gin, tequila, rum, crème de menthe, lemon juice and sugar syrup over ice cubes and shake vigorously until well frosted. Strain into a highball glass filled with cracked ice and top up with cola. Dress with a lime or lemon slice.

BRANDY JULEP ◄

SERVES 1

cracked ice

2 measures brandy

1 tsp sugar syrup

4 fresh mint leaves

fresh mint sprig

lemon slice

Fill a chilled lowball glass with cracked ice. Add the brandy, sugar syrup and mint leaves, and stir well to mix. Dress the cocktail with a sprig of fresh mint, a slice of lemon and a straw.

If you leave out the pineapple juice and wedge from the Cuban Special, it becomes a Cuban Sidecar – but don't, because the fruit turns it into a longer drink that's perfect for an afternoon in the sun.

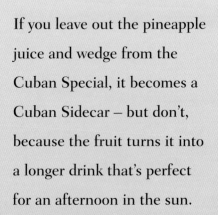

CUBAN SPECIAL ▲

SERVES 1

2 measures rum

1 measure lime juice

1 tbsp pineapple juice

1 tsp triple sec

pineapple wedge

Pour the rum, lime juice, pineapple juice and triple sec over ice cubes and shake until well frosted. Strain into a chilled cocktail glass and dress with a wedge of pineapple.

ROYAL WEDDING ▲

SERVES 1

1 measure kirsch

1 measure peach brandy

1 measure orange juice

Pour the kirsch, peach brandy and orange juice over ice cubes and shake vigorously until well frosted. Strain into a chilled cocktail glass.

PALM BEACH ▲

If it's been a long time since your last holiday, conjure up the blue skies and rolling surf of Florida with this sunny cocktail.

SERVES 1

cracked ice

1 measure white rum

1 measure gin

1 measure pineapple juice

pineapple leaves

Shake the rum, gin and pineapple juice vigorously over the cracked ice until well frosted. Pour into a chilled highball glass and decorate with pineapple leaves.

JOCOSE JULEP ▾

SERVES 1

4–6 ice cubes, crushed

3 measures bourbon whiskey

1 measure green crème de menthe

1½ measures lime juice

1 tsp sugar syrup

5 fresh mint leaves

cracked ice

sparkling water

fresh mint sprig

Put the crushed ice into a blender or food processor, add the bourbon, green crème de menthe, lime juice, sugar syrup and fresh mint leaves, and process until smooth. Fill a chilled lowball glass with the cracked ice and pour in the cocktail. Top up with sparkling water and stir gently to mix. Dress with a sprig of fresh mint.

It is said in Virginia that a julep, above all, is a state of mind. Considering that the word jocose means 'merry' – you get the general idea of of the Jocose Julep from its name.

BIRD OF PARADISE COOLER

SERVES 1

2 measures gin

1 measure lemon juice

1 tsp grenadine

1 tsp sugar syrup

1 egg white

cracked ice

sparkling water

Vigorously shake the gin, lemon juice, grenadine, sugar syrup and egg white over ice cubes until well frosted. Half fill a chilled lowball glass with the cracked ice and pour the cocktail over it. Top up with sparkling water.

AMBROSIA ◄

SERVES 1

1½ measures brandy

1½ measures apple brandy

½ tsp raspberry syrup

champagne, chilled

1 raspberry

Pour the brandy, apple brandy and raspberry syrup over ice cubes and shake vigorously until well frosted. Strain into a chilled wine glass. Top up with chilled champagne and dress with a raspberry.

PARADISE ►

SERVES 1

2 measures apricot brandy

1 measure gin

1½ measures orange juice

½ tsp grenadine

Pour the apricot brandy, gin, orange juice and grenadine over ice cubes and shake vigorously until well frosted. Strain into a chilled cocktail glass.

AMIGOS PIÑA COLADA ◂

SERVES 4
10–12 ice cubes, crushed
250 ml/8 fl oz rum
300 ml/10 fl oz pineapple juice
5 measures coconut cream
2 measures dark rum
2 measures single cream
pineapple wedges
cocktail cherries

Whizz the crushed ice in a blender with the rum, pineapple juice, coconut cream, dark rum and cream. Blend until smooth. Pour, without straining, into chilled lowball or hurricane glasses and decorate with wedges of pineapple and cocktail cherries.

GRAND BAHAMA ▸

SERVES 1
1 measure white rum
½ measure brandy
½ measure triple sec
1 measure lime juice
lime slice

Pour the white rum, brandy, triple sec and lime juice over ice cubes and shake vigorously until well frosted. Strain into a chilled cocktail glass. Serve with the slice of lime.

The classic Piña Colada, invented in the 1950s in Puerto Rico, usually uses light rum, pineapple juice and coconut cream. This version is stronger as it contains dark rum as well. The cream also makes it richer than the original.

CHICA CHICA ◂

SERVES 1
2 measures raspberry vodka
1 measure Chambéry (a type of white vermouth)
2 measures cranberry and raspberry juice
crushed ice
1 measure apple juice
lemonade
apple slices

Mix the raspberry vodka, Chambéry, cranberry and raspberry juice and crushed ice together in a chilled highball glass. Stir in the apple juice and top up with lemonade to taste. Finish with slices of apple.

It is easy to buy flavoured vodkas, but you can make your own. Add a small quantity of the flavouring – a few raspberries, blackcurrants, dried apricots, a piece of lime or lemon peel or even a piece of chilli – to a bottle of vodka and leave for 12 hours.

There are many variations on the Zombie, but they are generally a mix of three types of rum and various fruity libations. An exceptionally strong cocktail, the name comes from its obvious effect on the consumer.

KLONDIKE COOLER ‹

You can, of course, make this with a favourite whiskey if you have one.

SERVES 1
½ tsp caster sugar
1 measure ginger ale
cracked ice
2 measures blended whiskey
sparkling water
twist of lemon peel

Put the caster sugar into a chilled highball glass and add the ginger ale. Stir until the sugar has dissolved, then fill the glass with cracked ice. Pour the whiskey over the ice and top up with sparkling water. Stir gently to mix and dress with a twist of lemon peel.

WALKING ZOMBIE ▲

SERVES 1
1 measure white rum
1 measure golden rum
1 measure dark rum
1 measure apricot brandy
1 measure lime juice
1 measure pineapple juice
1 tsp sugar syrup
cracked ice
orange and lime slices

Pour the white, golden and dark rum, apricot brandy, lime juice, pineapple juice and sugar syrup over ice cubes. Shake vigorously until frosted. Half fill a chilled highball glass with the cracked ice and strain the cocktail over it. Dress with slices of orange and lime.

A.J. SHAKE ▸

As you'll realise from the list of ingredients, the 'A.J.' stands for applejack, but if you can't get that, apple brandy will do just as well.

SERVES 1
1½ measures applejack
1 measure grapefruit juice

Pour the applejack and grapefruit juice over ice cubes and shake vigorously until well frosted. Strain into a chilled cocktail glass.

SWEET SINGAPORE SLING ▴

SERVES 1
1 measure gin
2 measures cherry brandy
dash of lemon juice
cracked ice
soda water
cocktail cherry

Vigorously shake the gin, cherry brandy and a dash of lemon juice over ice cubes until well frosted. Half fill a chilled lowball glass with cracked ice and strain in the cocktail. Top up with soda water and decorate with a cocktail cherry.

The classic Singapore Sling is still served at the Raffles Hotel in Singapore, where it was invented by barman Ngiam Tong Boon in the early 20th century. The original contained Benedictine. But the cherry brandy in this refreshing variant ensures the drink retains its trademark rosy pink hue.

ZOMBIE PRINCE ◄

SERVES 1

dash of Angostura bitters

1 measure white rum

1 measure golden rum

1 measure dark rum

½ measure lemon juice

½ measure orange juice

½ measure grapefruit juice

1 tsp brown sugar

Splash the Angostura bitters over ice cubes in a mixing glass, pour in the white rum, golden rum, dark rum, lemon juice, orange juice and grapefruit juice, and add the brown sugar. Stir to mix well, then strain into a chilled highball glass.

SEX ON THE BEACH

Holiday drinks are often long and fruity and this refreshing cocktail is designed to make you reminisce about happy days in the sun.

SERVES 1

1 measure peach schnapps

1 measure vodka

2 measures fresh orange juice

3 measures cranberry and peach juice

crushed ice

dash of lemon juice

orange peel

Shake the peach schnapps, vodka, orange juice, and cranberry and peach juice over ice cubes until well frosted. Strain into a highball glass filled with crushed ice and squeeze over the lemon juice. Dress with orange peel.

WHITE LION ▲

SERVES 1

4–6 ice cubes, cracked

dash of Angostura bitters

dash of grenadine

2 measures white rum

1 measure lemon juice

1 tsp sugar syrup

Shake the cracked ice in a cocktail shaker with the Angostura bitters, grenadine, white rum, lemon juice and sugar syrup until a frost forms. Strain into a chilled cocktail glass.

TEQUILA FIZZ ▸

A fizz usually contains a spirit and at least one fruit juice, and is topped up with a fizzy soft drink. Fizzes are always shaken rather than mixed.

SERVES 1
3 measures white tequila
1 measure grenadine
1 measure lime juice
1 egg white
cracked ice
ginger ale

Pour the white tequila, grenadine, lime juice and egg white over ice cubes and shake vigorously until well frosted. Half fill a chilled highball or lowball glass with cracked ice and strain the cocktail over it. Top up with ginger ale.

BELLE COLLINS

SERVES 1
3 fresh mint sprigs
4–6 ice cubes, crushed
2 measures gin
1 measure lemon juice
1 tsp sugar syrup
sparkling water

Crush two of the sprigs of fresh mint and place them in a chilled highball glass. Add the crushed ice and pour in the gin, lemon juice and sugar syrup. Top up with sparkling water, stir gently and decorate with the remaining mint sprig.

COUNTRY COUSIN COLLINS ▶

Despite its name, there are definitely no flies on this member of the Collins family.

SERVES 1

2 measures apple brandy

1 measure lemon juice

½ tsp sugar syrup

crushed ice

dash of orange bitters

sparkling water

lemon slices

Blend the apple brandy, lemon juice and sugar syrup with crushed ice and a dash of orange bitters at medium speed for ten seconds. Pour into a chilled lowball glass and top up with sparkling water. Stir gently and dress with lemon slices.

MAGNA CARTA ▶

If you really want to lounge around in style, you can use champagne rather than sparkling wine to finish this cocktail off.

SERVES 1

lime wedge

caster sugar

2 measures white tequila

1 measure triple sec

sparkling wine or champagne, chilled

Rub the rim of a wine or highball glass with the wedge of lime and then dip the glass in caster sugar to frost it. Over ice cubes, stir the white tequila and triple sec together in a mixing glass. Strain into the prepared glass and top up with chilled sparkling wine.

END OF THE ROAD ▸

SERVES 1
3 measures gin
1 measure crème de menthe
1 measure pastis
cracked ice
sprig of mint
soda water

Stir the gin, crème de menthe and pastis together over ice cubes. Strain into a highball glass filled with cracked ice and dress with a sprig of mint. Top up with soda water, unless you feel like a shorter drink.

SEABREEZE

Pink grapefruit juice is much sweeter and subtler than its paler cousin, so it's ideal for cocktails where you want just a slight sharpness.

SERVES 1
1½ measures vodka
½ measure cranberry juice
pink grapefruit juice

Pour the vodka and cranberry juice over ice cubes and shake until frosted. Pour into a chilled highball glass and top up with pink grapefruit juice to taste.

COSTA DEL SOL ▸

SERVES 1
2 measures gin
1 measure apricot brandy
1 measure triple sec

Pour the gin, apricot brandy and triple sec over ice cubes and shake vigorously until well frosted. Strain into a chilled cocktail glass or lowball glass.

BLACK AND TAN ▸

SERVES 1
150 ml/5 fl oz ginger ale, chilled
150 ml/5 fl oz ginger beer, chilled
lime slice

*Pour the ginger ale into a chilled lowball glass, then add
the ginger beer. Do not stir, but dress with a slice of lime.*

FROZEN STRAWBERRY DAIQUIRI ◂

SERVES 1
crushed ice
2 measures white rum
1 measure lime juice
1 tsp sugar syrup
7 strawberries

*Whizz the crushed ice in a blender and then add
the white rum, lime juice, sugar syrup and six of the
strawberries. Blend until slushy. Pour the concoction
into a chilled cocktail glass and dress with the
remaining strawberry.*

Not to be confused with the lager/stout or beer/stout drink of the same name, the stark contrast in this lighter and more refreshing Black and Tan comes from the pairing of non-alcoholic ginger ale and alcoholic ginger beer.

MIAMI BEACH ◄

SERVES 1

2 measures Scotch whisky

1½ measures dry vermouth

2 measures grapefruit juice

twist of orange peel

Pour the Scotch, dry vermouth and grapefruit juice over ice cubes. Shake vigorously until well frosted, then strain into a chilled cocktail glass and serve with the twist of orange peel.

PALM BEACH SOUR

SERVES 1

⅓ measure gin

⅓ measure grapefruit juice

⅙ measure dry vermouth

2–3 drops Angostura bitters

1 tsp caster sugar

1 egg white

Shake the gin, grapefruit juice, dry vermouth, Angostura bitters, sugar and egg white with ice cubes. Strain into a chilled cocktail glass or wine glass.

HALLEY'S COMFORT ►

SERVES 1

cracked ice

2 measures Southern Comfort

2 measures peach schnapps

sparkling water

lemon slice

Half fill a chilled lowball glass or highball glass with the cracked ice. Pour the Southern Comfort and peach schnapps over the ice and top up with sparkling water. Stir gently and dress with a slice of lemon.

THE FLATIRON LOUNGE

NEW YORK CITY

Like a good cocktail there are a number of ingredients that make a good bar. The Flatiron Lounge in New York City is a perfect example. Situated near the historic Flatiron Building (why not admire the architecture and then retire to the Lounge for a drink), this bar has a cool Art Deco interior with dark red leatherette banquettes and cobalt blue mirrors. Opened in 2003, this classy joint marks a relaxed return to the luxurious abandon of the bygone classic cocktail era of the 1920s. The meticulously restored Art Deco bar was once lent on by Frank Sinatra and the Rat Pack at New York's legendary Manhattan Ballroom.

But it's the cocktails that make this one of the world's best bars. It has a unique menu of modern, tasty cocktails that all contain the

BEST FOR

classic cocktails in Art Deco splendour

LONG ISLAND GREEN TEA

SERVES 4

115 g/4 oz fine sugar
125 ml/4½ fl oz hot water
250 ml/9 fl oz fresh lemon juice
750 ml bottle sake
10 green tea bags
150 ml/5 fl oz premium gin
150 ml/5 fl oz premium
 lemon vodka
4 tsp grenadine
8 brandied cherries

Make a sour mix by dissolving the sugar in the hot water, add the lemon juice and chill. Warm the sake by immersing the bottle in hot water. Decant the sake into a bowl, add the tea bags and steep for 40 minutes. Strain the sake mixture into a jug. Stir in the sour mix, gin and vodka. Fill four tall glasses with ice. Pour the mixture over the ice, adding one teaspoon of grenadine to each glass. Serve with two brandied cherries on a stick.

❖

'A good cocktail should give you more than a buzz, it should lift you up and take you someplace else.'

Julie Reiner, mixologist and co-owner of the Flatiron Lounge

perfect blend of alcohol and exotic fresh ingredients. These drinks are like art in a glass. The menu changes seasonally and there are specials available, depending on what's available. The menu is truly unique and full of house-made infusions like Harvest Punch (vodka steeped in Pacific Rim teas, flavoured with passion flower and mint), or Juniper Breeze (a fresh mix of Plymouth gin, elderflower cordial, grapefruit, lime and cranberry) and guest cocktails from the finest mixologists in the city.

In a city of a thousand bars (and more) this is a special place. The drinks come as they should: surprising, varied, fresh, full of flavour and demanding to be sipped and savoured. Tip: try the 'flight of the day' where you can have your tastebuds transported to anywhere in the world on board a trio of miniature cocktails served on a custom-made wooden tray.

FLATIRON LOUNGE

Flatiron Building
37 West 19th Street
(between 5th and 6th Avenue)
NY 10011
USA
+1 212 727 7741
www.flatironlounge.com

Open daily
Sunday to Wednesday
5.00 p.m to 2.00 a.m.
Thursday, Friday and Saturday
5.00 p.m. to 4.00 a.m.

BEFORE DINNER

Sometimes it's hard to know what to drink before you eat. You certainly don't want to approach dinner feeling bloated and sluggish. Indeed, an aperitif should sharpen your appetite, not kill it. So think carefully about what you order. Thankfully, however you decide to prime your palette, there is a cocktail here for you.

COSMOPOLITAN ‹

This fashionable cocktail, made famous by the TV show *Sex and the City*, is ideal before a sophisticated dinner party.

SERVES 1
2 measures vodka
1 measure triple sec
1 measure fresh lime juice
1 measure cranberry juice
twist of orange peel

Shake the vodka, triple sec, lime juice and cranberry juice over ice cubes until well frosted. Strain into a chilled cocktail glass and dress with a twist of orange peel.

Although a relative newcomer to the scene, having arrived sometime in the mid-1980s, probably from Miami's fashionable South Beach, the Cosmopolitan – or Cosmo, as those who imbibe it frequently call it – has rapidly established itself as a classic cocktail.

In part this may be due to its subsequent association with New York's Manhattan, but the Cosmopolitan is also ideal before a dinner party in slightly more humble surroundings.

In its initial incarnation, the cranberry juice was present to give the merest hint of pink, but most recipes now include a good dose of cranberry, which imparts a rich, almost red colour, and gently undercuts the citrussy combination of the orange-flavoured triple sec and the lime.

Whatever spirits it utilises, the key ingredient of a Sour, as the name suggests, is citrus juice. It is usually served in a sour or a cocktail glass and garnished with a maraschino cherry, though on the rocks in a lowball glass will be fine.

ITALIAN STALLION ▾

SERVES 1
4–6 ice cubes
dash of Angostura bitters
2 measures bourbon
1 measure Campari
½ measure sweet vermouth
twist of lemon peel

Put the ice cubes into a mixing glass, add a dash of Angostura and pour in the bourbon, Campari and sweet vermouth. Stir well to mix, then strain into a chilled cocktail glass and dress with a twist of lemon peel.

BOSTON SOUR ◂

SERVES 1
1 measure lemon or lime juice
2 measures blended whiskey
1 egg white
1 tsp caster sugar or syrup de gomme
lemon slice
cocktail cherry

Shake the lemon or lime juice, whiskey, egg white and sugar over ice cubes and strain into a cocktail glass or sour glass. Finish with a slice of lemon and a cocktail cherry.

BELLINITINI ▸

A lovely variation on one of the best-known aperitifs – just peachy.

SERVES 1
2 measures vodka
1 measure peach schnapps
1 measure peach juice
champagne, chilled

Pour the vodka, peach schnapps and peach juice over ice cubes and shake vigorously until well frosted. Strain into a chilled wine glass or flute and top up with the chilled champagne.

BELLINI

This delicious concoction was created by Giuseppe Cipriani at Harry's Bar in Venice, around 1943.

SERVES 1
1 measure fresh peach juice made from lightly
   sweetened liquidised peaches
caster sugar
3 measures champagne, chilled

Dip the rim of a chilled flute into some peach juice and then into the sugar to create a sugar-frosted effect. Set the glass aside to dry. Pour the peach juice into the flute, carefully top up with the champagne and stir gently.

APPLE MARTINI ▸

Very much a cocktail of the moment, the Apple Martini, or Appletini as it's also known, is smooth and very easy to drink. Sour apple schnapps instead of ordinary apple schnapps will enhance the sharpness, as will a splash of lemon juice. If you have apple purée to hand you can use that instead of the apple juice or substitute still cider to increase the alcohol content.

SERVES 1
cracked ice
1 measure vodka
1 measure apple schnapps
1 measure apple juice
2 thin slices of apple

Pour the vodka, apple schnapps and apple juice over cracked ice and shake until well frosted. Strain into a chilled cocktail glass and dress with slices of apple.

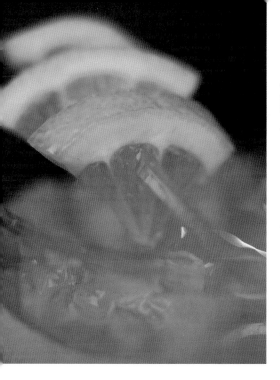

JUAN COLLINS ◄

Another member of the Collins family – this one may hail from down Mexico way.

SERVES 1
cracked ice
2 measures white tequila
1 measure lemon juice
1 tsp sugar syrup
sparkling mineral water
lemon slice

Half fill a chilled highball glass with cracked ice and pour in the white tequila, lemon juice and sugar syrup. Top up with sparkling mineral water and stir gently. Dress with a slice of lemon.

BACK TO THE FUTURE ◄

SERVES 1
2 measures gin
1 measure slivovitz
1 measure lemon juice
twist of lemon peel

Pour the gin, slivovitz and lemon juice over ice cubes and shake vigorously until well frosted. Strain into a chilled cocktail glass and serve with the twist of lemon peel.

DEPTH CHARGE

When an anise-based spirit such as Pernod is mixed with water it turns the water cloudy, but the same doesn't happen when it's mixed with other spirits – until the ice starts melting...

SERVES 1
1 measure gin
1 measure Lillet
2 dashes Pernod

Pour the gin, Lillet and Pernod over ice cubes and shake until well frosted, then strain into a chilled cocktail glass with one or two ice cubes.

MOSCOW MULE

The name of this cocktail derives from its principal ingredient, vodka, which comes from Russia, hence 'Moscow', and has something of a kick, hence 'Mule'.

SERVES 1
2 measures vodka
1 measure lime juice
cracked ice
ginger beer
lime slice

Pour the vodka and lime juice over ice cubes and shake vigorously until well frosted. Half fill a chilled highball glass with cracked ice and strain the cocktail over it. Top up with ginger beer and dress with a slice of lime.

The Moscow Mule was invented in the 1950s when a barman at the Cock 'n' Bull in Hollywood discovered he'd ordered too many crates of ginger beer. So he mixed it with vodka and inadvertently created a classic. The drink became so popular that it kicked off a craze for 'white whiskey', as vodka was known at the time.

COLLEEN ▲

SERVES 1
2 measures Irish whiskey
1 measure Irish Mist
1 measure triple sec
1 tsp lemon juice

Pour the Irish whiskey, Irish Mist, triple sec and lemon juice over ice cubes and shake vigorously until well frosted. Strain into a chilled cocktail glass.

MONTGOMERY

SERVES 1

3 measures gin or vodka

1 tsp vermouth

olive or lemon zest

Pour the gin and vermouth over ice cubes, strain into a
chilled cocktail glass and add an olive or a little lemon
zest.

ROLLS-ROYCE

SERVES 1

4–6 ice cubes

3 measures gin

1 measure dry vermouth

1 measure sweet vermouth

¼ tsp Benedictine

Put the ice cubes into a mixing glass. Pour the gin, dry
vermouth, sweet vermouth and Benedictine over them,
stir well to mix and then strain into a chilled cocktail glass.

BRANDY OLD FASHIONED ◄

SERVES 1
1 sugar cube
dash of Angostura bitters
1 tsp water
3 measures brandy
cracked ice
twist of lemon peel

*Place the sugar cube in a small, chilled old-fashioned or
lowball glass, and add the Angostura bitters and water.
Mash with a spoon until the sugar has dissolved, then
pour in the brandy and stir. Add the cracked ice and
decorate with a twist of lemon peel.*

The Old Fashioned is such
a ubiquitous cocktail that a
small, straight-sided tumbler
or lowball glass is also known
as an 'old-fashioned' glass.
This version of the cocktail is
based on brandy, rather than
bourbon or whiskey.

VICTORY ▲

SERVES 1
2 measures Pernod
1 measure grenadine
sparkling mineral water

*Pour the Pernod and grenadine over ice cubes and
shake vigorously until well frosted. Strain into a chilled
highball glass and top up with sparkling mineral water.*

ROSITA ▶

SERVES 1

4–6 ice cubes

2 measures Campari

2 measures white tequila

½ measure dry vermouth

½ measure sweet vermouth

twist of lime peel

*Put the ice cubes into a mixing glass and pour the
Campari, white tequila, and dry and sweet vermouths
over them. Stir well to mix, then strain into a chilled lowball
glass and dress with a twist of lime peel.*

THE BENTLEY ▲

Champagne cocktails tend to get better and better the
more you drink...

SERVES 1

½ measure cognac or brandy

½ measure peach liqueur, peach brandy or schnapps

juice of 1 passion fruit, sieved

1 ice cube

champagne, chilled

*Mix the cognac, peach liqueur and passion fruit juice
gently together in a chilled highball glass. Add the single
ice cube and slowly pour in champagne to taste.*

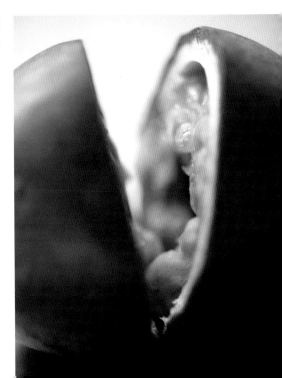

TNT

SERVES 1

4–6 ice cubes, cracked

1 measure Pernod

1 measure rye whiskey

Put the cracked ice into a mixing glass and pour the Pernod and rye whiskey over them. Stir well to mix and strain into a chilled cocktail glass.

BRANDY SOUR ◄

First made in the American south in the mid-19th century, sours were based on brandy, but as distilled French wines became harder to come by, American whiskey replaced it as the spirit of choice. Here the brandy is reinstated.

SERVES 1

1 measure lemon or lime juice

2½ measures brandy

1 tsp caster sugar or syrup de gomme

lemon or lime slice

maraschino cherry

Shake the lemon juice, brandy and sugar well over ice cubes and strain into a cocktail glass or sour glass. Finish with a slice of lemon and a maraschino cherry.

ORANGE GIN SLING

SERVES 1

2 measures gin

4 dashes orange bitters

Pour the gin into a cocktail glass then carefully splash on the orange bitters.

DUCHESS ▾

SERVES 1

4–6 ice cubes, cracked

1 measure Pernod

1 measure sweet vermouth

1 measure dry vermouth

Put the cracked ice into a mixing glass. Pour the Pernod, sweet vermouth and dry vermouth over the ice, stir well to mix and then strain the mixture into a chilled cocktail glass or lowball glass.

GRAND DUCHESS ▴

SERVES 1

10 ice cubes, cracked

2 measures vodka

1 measure triple sec

3 measures cranberry juice

2 measures orange juice

Put half the cracked ice cubes into a mixing glass. Pour the vodka, triple sec, cranberry juice and orange juice over the ice and stir well to mix. Half fill a chilled lowball glass with the rest of the cracked ice and strain the cocktail over it.

ADAM 'N' EVE

SERVES 1

2 measures triple sec

1 measure vodka

1 measure grapefruit juice

1 measure cranberry juice

5–6 cubes pineapple

2 tsp caster sugar

2 tbsp crushed ice

strawberry slice

Shake the triple sec, vodka, grapefruit juice and cranberry juice over ice cubes until well frosted and strain the mixture into a chilled highball glass. In a blender, whizz the pineapple with the sugar and the crushed ice until you have a frothy slush. Float this gently on the top of the cocktail and dress it with a slice of strawberry.

The base of the Adam 'n' Eve is sharp and astringent, while the top is sweet and frothy – it's a brilliant combination, but watch you don't lose your fig leaf.

CONFEDERATE RAILROAD ▲

SERVES 1

2 measures bourbon

1 measure Southern Comfort

1 measure orange juice

dash of triple sec

orange slice

Pour the bourbon, Southern Comfort, orange juice and a dash of triple sec over ice cubes and shake vigorously until well frosted. Strain into a chilled cocktail glass and dress with the slice of orange.

ALLIGATOR ◄

SERVES 1
2 measures vodka
1 measure Midori
½ measure dry vermouth
¼ tsp lemon juice
green melon balls

Pour the vodka, Midori, dry vermouth and lemon juice over ice cubes and shake vigorously until well frosted. Strain into a chilled cocktail glass and serve with green melon balls on a cocktail stick.

MIMOSA

This drink apparently acquired its name because it is the same colour as the attractive yellow bloom of a mimosa.

SERVES 1
juice of 1 passion fruit
½ measure orange curaçao
crushed ice
champagne, chilled
star fruit slice
twist of orange peel

Scoop out the passion fruit flesh into a jug or shaker and shake with the curaçao and a little crushed ice until frosted. Pour into the base of a champagne flute and top up with champagne. Dress with the star fruit and a twist of orange peel.

THIRD DEGREE ►

SERVES 1
4–6 ice cubes, cracked
dash of Pernod
2 measures gin
1 measure dry vermouth
twist of lemon peel

Put cracked ice into a mixing glass. Dash Pernod over the ice and pour in the gin and the dry vermouth. Stir well to mix then strain into a chilled cocktail glass and serve with a twist of lemon peel.

STOCKHOLM

SERVES 1
1 sugar cube
2 measures lemon vodka
1 measure lemon juice
sparkling wine, chilled

Put the sugar cube in a wine glass with the lemon vodka and lemon juice. Stir to dissolve the sugar and top up with chilled sparkling wine.

CHELSEA SIDECAR ▲

So strong are this cocktail's associations with the famous artists' and writers' hangout in New York that it's sometimes known as a Chelsea Hotel.

SERVES 1
2 measures gin
1 measure triple sec
1 measure lemon juice
twist of lemon peel

Pour the gin, triple sec and lemon juice over ice cubes and shake vigorously until well frosted. Strain into a chilled cocktail glass and dress with a twist of lemon peel.

WEDDING BELLS ▶

SERVES 1
4–6 ice cubes, cracked
dash of orange bitters
2 measures rye whiskey
1 measure triple sec
2 measures Lillet
twist of orange peel

Put the cracked ice into a mixing glass. Dash orange bitters over the ice and pour in the rye whiskey, triple sec and Lillet. Stir well to mix, then strain into a chilled cocktail glass and serve with a twist of orange peel.

MANHATTAN ‹

It is thought that this drink originated at the Manhattan Club in New York City in the early 1870s, where it was invented for a banquet hosted by Jennie Jerome (mother of British prime minister Winston Churchill) in honour of presidential candidate Samuel J. Tilden.

SERVES 1
cracked ice
dash of Angostura bitters
3 measures rye whiskey
1 measure sweet vermouth
cocktail cherry

In a mixing glass, stir the Angostura bitters, whiskey and vermouth together over cracked ice and mix well. Strain into a chilled cocktail glass or lowball glass and decorate with a cocktail cherry.

In the movie *Some Like it Hot*, starring Marilyn Monroe and Jack Lemmon, the girls throw an impromptu party on the train during which they pool their smuggled alcohol to make Manhattans. They mention using bourbon whiskey rather than Canadian, and mix the cocktail in a hot water bottle.

TIGER BY THE TAIL ▲

SERVES 1
2 measures Pernod
4 measures orange juice
¼ tsp triple sec
crushed ice
twist of lime peel

Blend the Pernod, orange juice and triple sec with the crushed ice until smooth. Pour into a chilled wine glass and dress with a twist of lime peel.

BOURBON SOUR ▾

Sours, which can be made with vodka, gin or other spirits, as well as brandy and whiskey, are always shaken and should be served in a special sour glass, although, if you don't have one, a highball or old-fashioned glass works equally well.

SERVES 1
1 measure lemon or lime juice
2 measures bourbon
1 tsp caster sugar or syrup de gomme
orange slice

Shake the lemon juice, bourbon and sugar well over ice cubes and strain into a cocktail glass or sour glass. Finish with a slice of orange.

WHITE LADY

Simple, elegant, subtle and much more powerful than its appearance may suggest, this is the perfect cocktail to serve before an al fresco summer dinner.

SERVES 1
cracked ice
2 measures gin
1 measure triple sec
1 measure lemon juice

Pour the gin, triple sec and lemon juice over the cracked ice and shake vigorously until well frosted. Strain into a chilled cocktail glass.

SAPPHIRE MARTINI ▸

SERVES 1
4–6 ice cubes, cracked
2 measures gin
½ measure blue curaçao
cocktail cherry

Put the cracked ice into a mixing glass and pour the gin and blue curaçao over it. Stir well to mix then strain into a chilled cocktail glass. Dress with a cocktail cherry.

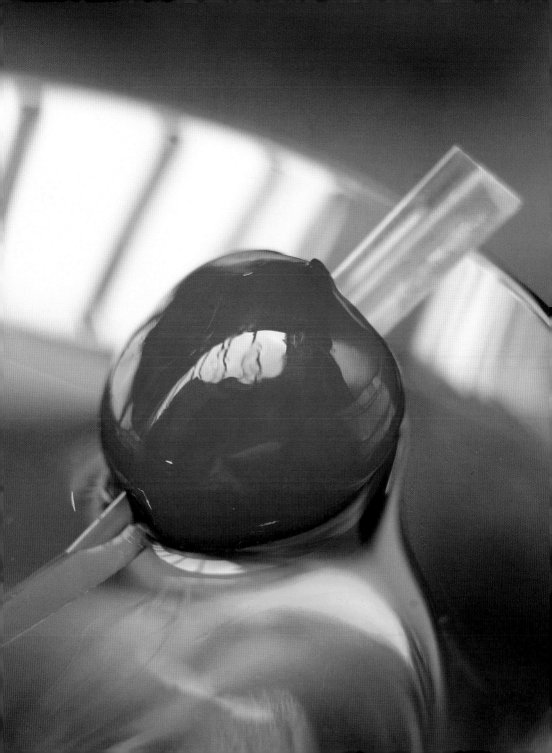

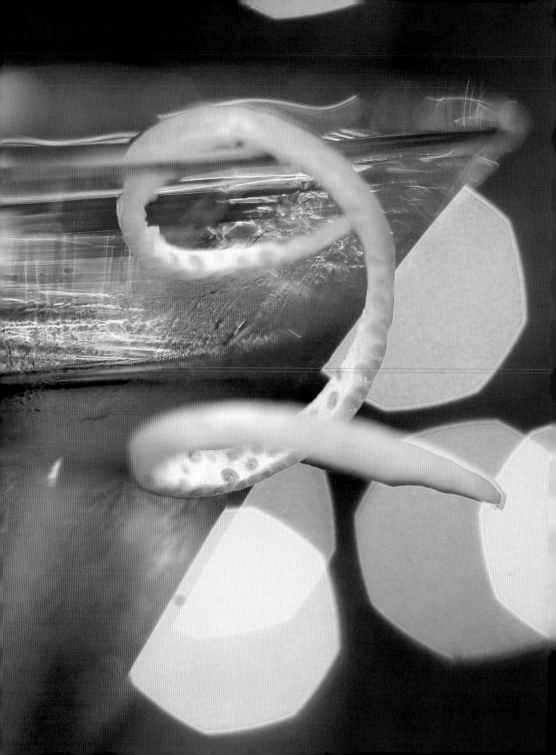

TOPAZ MARTINI ◀

SERVES 1
4–6 ice cubes, cracked
2 measures gin
½ measure orange curaçao
lemon slice
twist of orange or lemon peel

*Put the cracked ice into a mixing glass and pour the
gin and orange curaçao over it. Stir well to mix then
strain into a chilled cocktail glass. Dress with a twist
of orange peel.*

KIR

SERVES 1
½ tsp crème de cassis
white wine, chilled
twist of lemon peel

*Pour the crème de cassis into a chilled wine glass and
top up with the wine. Stir well, run a twist of lemon peel
around the rim of the glass, squeeze and drop it in.*

LONDON FRENCH 75 ▲

The classic French 75 cocktail can be made with
a number of spirits, but is always topped up with
champagne. This version uses London gin.

SERVES 1
2 measures London gin
1 measure lemon juice
champagne, chilled

*Pour the gin and lemon juice over ice cubes and shake
vigorously until well frosted. Strain into a chilled wine glass
and top up with chilled champagne. If you want to make
it look better you could dress it with a cocktail cherry.*

GRAND ROYAL CLOVER CLUB ▸

SERVES 1
2 measures gin
1 measure lemon juice
1 measure grenadine
1 egg white
twist of lemon peel

Pour the gin, lemon juice, grenadine and egg white over ice cubes. Shake vigorously until well frosted. Strain into a chilled cocktail glass and serve with a twist of lemon peel.

CORDLESS SCREWDRIVER ▲

A shorter, shooter-style version of the famous Screwdriver (page 296), this gives an instant buzz.

SERVES 1
orange wedges
caster sugar
2 measures vodka, chilled

Rub the rim of a chilled shot glass with an orange wedge and dip into some caster sugar to create a sugar-frosted effect. Pour the chilled vodka into the glass. Dip a wedge of orange into caster sugar. Down the vodka in one go and suck the orange.

Groucho Marx is well known for claiming that he wouldn't want to belong to any club that was prepared to accept him as a member. The Grand Royal Clover Club is unlikely to have any shortage of willing members.

CITY SPACE BAR

MOSCOW

Many visitors arrive in the Russian capital without appreciating how colossal it is. It is one thing to know that this is Europe's largest city by far, but it's another matter entirely to clap eyes on it. Yet up here on the 34th floor of the tastefully minimalist Swissôtel Krasne Holmy, the world's most gaudily excessive, exciting, monolithic, gridlocked, enigmatic, chaotic, go-ahead and contradictory metropolis is laid out sprawling at your feet.

Leaving rivals like the 25th-floor Sky Lounge and 27-storey Red Bar in the shade, the central City Space Bar is now the place to come to watch the sun set – only temporarily, mind – on the resurgent Russian empire. City Space offers a truly panoramic

BEST FOR

watching the sun set

ISAEV

This is a Russian version of the classic James Bond vodka martini. Devised by City Space Bar's award-winning bartender and consultant mixologist, Alexander Kan, it is named after a famous Russian spy, Maxim Isaev (codename Shtirlitz), who worked in Germany during the Second World War. The drink distinguishes itself by replacing the standard ingredient of dry vermouth with birch juice. Although nowadays valued for its detoxifying effects, birch juice, made from silver birch trees, is a traditional and widely available Russian speciality. The premium juice served at the City Space Bar is freshly distilled in-house.

SERVES 1
2 measures vodka
1 measure birch juice

Shake vodka and birch juice reduction together with ice cubes in a mixing glass. Strain into a chilled cocktail glass. Garnish with a twist of lemon.

'Although we aim to deliver unique concoctions of flavours, a successful bar also has to deliver excellent customer service.'

Manager, Bek Narzibekov

360-degree view that includes the Kremlin, St Basil's Cathedral, the Moskva River, the resurrected Church of Christ the Saviour and the endless Moscow suburbs.

The entrance to the bar is dramatic too. Guests emerge from the lift on the 33rd floor and rise into the middle of the bar's space-age glass bowl via a black spiral staircase. Here they're in a heady world, with a cocktail list presided over by manager Bek Narzibekov, who was part of the team at London's fabled Milk & Honey when it was named Best UK Bar. A honeyed Bloody Mary is just one of the innovative specialities on offer.

This being Moscow as it goes through its hottest-city-on-the-planet phase, footing the bill is also a breathtaking experience, but a trip to the Russian capital just wouldn't be complete without saying 'na zdarovye' here.

CITY SPACE BAR
Kosmodamianskaya naberezhnaya 52
Building 6
115054 Moscow
Russia
+7 495 787 9800
www.swissotel.com/moscow

Open daily
7.00 p.m. to 3.00 a.m.

IN THE MOOD

Any time, any place, anywhere – the words of the old Martini advertising slogan can't really be bettered. And for those immutable moments when you just must have a drink, when you need to stimulate your senses and tantalise your taste buds, here's an exemplary selection of classic and contemporary cocktails.

THE ULTIMATE CLASSIC MARTINI ◄

Where to begin? For many this is the ultimate mixed drink. More words have been written about the Martini than about any other cocktail.

SERVES 1
cracked ice
3 measures vodka or gin
1 tsp dry vermouth or to taste
green cocktail olive

Shake the vodka and vermouth over cracked ice until well frosted. Strain into a chilled martini or cocktail glass and dress with a cocktail olive.

The simple fact is that the drink does not get its name from the popular Italian brand of vermouth. It may have been named after the town of Martinez in California, which claims to be the drink's birthplace, or after would-be inventor Martini di Arma di Taggia, who was a New York hotel barman. But no one is completely sure. What is definitely true, however, is that the Martini was originally made with gin, but is now more often than not made with vodka.

Whatever spirit you use, though, make sure it is icy cold, and chill the glass – obviously a Martini glass with its flared cup and elegant stem – too.

There are multitudinous variations on its basic theme, some of which are featured elsewhere in this book.

THE MODERN MARTINI ▾

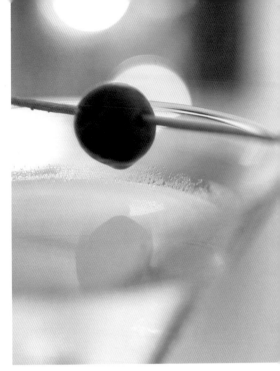

Other good fruits to try with this recipe are kiwi, cranberry, pear and watermelon.

SERVES 1
1 very ripe pomegranate
2 measures vodka or gin
dash of sugar syrup

Spoon the flesh of the pomegranate into a shaker and lightly crush or muddle. Add the vodka and sugar syrup, and shake well over ice cubes. Strain into an iced martini or cocktail glass.

DIRTY MARTINI ▴

SERVES 1
3 measures gin
1 measure dry vermouth
½ measure brine from a jar of cocktail olives
cocktail olive

Vigorously shake the gin, dry vermouth and cocktail olive brine over ice cubes until well frosted. Strain into a chilled martini or cocktail glass and dress with a cocktail olive.

THE LEGEND MARTINI

SERVES 1
2 measures vodka, iced
1 measure crème de mûre
1 measure fresh lime juice
dash of sugar syrup

Shake the iced vodka, crème de mûre, fresh lime juice and a dash of sugar syrup together over ice cubes until really well frosted. Strain into an iced martini or cocktail glass.

VIRGIN'S PRAYER ▲

SERVES 1
1 measure white rum
1 measure dark rum
1 measure Kahlúa
1 tsp lemon juice
2 tsp orange juice
lime slice

Vigorously shake the white rum, dark rum, Kahlúa, lemon juice and orange juice over ice cubes until well frosted. Strain into a chilled lowball glass. Dress with a slice of lime.

TOM COLLINS

Although invented in London in the early 1800s by a man called John Collins, this celebrated cocktail was commonly made with Old Tom gin and hence its name changed over time to Tom Collins.

SERVES 1
3 measures gin
2 measures lemon juice
½ measure sugar syrup
soda water
lemon slice

Pour the gin, lemon juice and sugar syrup over ice cubes and shake vigorously until well frosted. Strain into a chilled highball glass, top up with the soda water and dress with a slice of lemon.

BELLINI MARTINI ▶

SERVES 1

1 measure gin

½ measure brandy

½ measure peach purée

splash of sweet vermouth

peach slice

*Shake the gin, brandy, peach purée and sweet
vermouth over ice cubes until well frosted. Strain into
an iced martini or cocktail glass and dress with a
slice of peach.*

FIFTY FIFTY ▲

This is the original version of the Martini, using equal
measures of gin and vermouth.

SERVES 1

1 measure gin

1 measure dry vermouth

cocktail olive

*Shake the gin and dry vermouth over ice cubes until
well frosted. Strain into a chilled cocktail glass. Drop in
a cocktail olive and serve.*

SILVER BERRY

This drink is perfect for a special occasion, although
you really can't drink very many.

SERVES 1

1 measure raspberry vodka, iced

1 measure crème de cassis, iced

1 measure Cointreau, iced

edible silver paper or frozen berry

*Carefully and slowly layer the vodka, crème de cassis
and Cointreau, in that order, into a well-iced shot glass
or tall thin cocktail glass. The alcohol must be well iced
first and may need time to settle into layers. Dress with the
silver paper.*

DAIQUIRI

Daiquiri is a town in Cuba, where this drink was said to have been invented in the early part of the 20th century.

SERVES 1
cracked ice
2 measures white rum
¾ measure lime juice
½ tsp sugar syrup

Pour the rum, lime juice and sugar syrup over craked ice and shake vigorously until well frosted. Strain into a chilled cocktail glass.

GOLDEN FROG

Classic vodka cocktails were often intended to provide an alcoholic drink with no tell-tale signs on the breath, so they were usually fairly simple mixes with non-alcoholic flavours. Contemporary vodka cocktails, however, often include other spirits.

SERVES 1
4–6 ice cubes
1 measure vodka
1 measure Strega
1 measure Galliano
1 measure lemon juice

Whizz the ice cubes in a blender with the vodka, Strega, Galliano and lemon juice. Blend until slushy and pour into a chilled cocktail glass.

GIBSON ▶

SERVES 1
cracked ice
3 measures gin
1 tsp dry vermouth
2–3 cocktail onions

Put the cracked ice into a mixing glass, pour the gin and vermouth over it and stir well to mix. Strain into a chilled cocktail glass and dress with cocktail onions.

HAWAIIAN ORANGE BLOSSOM ◀

SERVES 1
2 measures gin
1 measure triple sec
2 measures orange juice
1 measure pineapple juice
pineapple wedge and leaf

Vigorously shake the gin, triple sec, orange juice and pineapple juice over ice cubes until well frosted. Strain into a chilled wine glass. Serve dressed with a pineapple wedge and leaf.

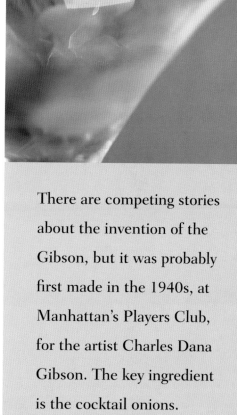

There are competing stories about the invention of the Gibson, but it was probably first made in the 1940s, at Manhattan's Players Club, for the artist Charles Dana Gibson. The key ingredient is the cocktail onions.

FAIR LADY ▶

SERVES 1
2 measures gin
1 measure orange juice
1 measure lime juice
1 egg white
dash of strawberry liqueur
1 strawberry
twist of lime peel

Vigorously shake the gin, orange juice, lime juice, egg white and strawberry liqueur over ice cubes until well frosted. Strain into a chilled cocktail glass. Serve with a slice of strawberry and a twist of lime peel.

BLUE BIRD ▲

SERVES 1
cracked ice
3 measures gin
1 measure blue curaçao
dash of Angostura bitters

Vigorously shake the gin, blue curaçao and Angostura bitters over cracked ice until well frosted. Strain into a chilled cocktail or wine glass.

HARVEY WALLBANGER

This well-known contemporary classic cocktail is great at parties, but at any other time too.

SERVES 1
3 measures vodka
8 measures orange juice
2 tsp Galliano
cherry
orange slice

Half fill a highball glass with ice cubes, pour the vodka and orange over the ice, and float the Galliano on top. Garnish with a cherry and slice of orange. For a warming variant, mix a splash of ginger wine with the vodka and orange.

POLYNESIAN SOUR ‹

SERVES 1
4–6 ice cubes, crushed
2 measures light rum
½ measure guava juice
½ measure lemon juice
½ measure orange juice

Whizz the crushed ice in a blender with the light rum, guava juice, lemon juice and orange juice until smooth. Pour the mixture into a chilled cocktail glass.

MINT JULEP

The Mint Julep is the traditional drink of the Kentucky Derby, a horse race that has been held annually in Louisville, Kentucky, since 1875.

SERVES 1
2 fresh mint sprigs
1 tbsp sugar syrup
crushed ice
3 measures bourbon whiskey

Put the leaves of one sprig of fresh mint and the sugar syrup into a chilled highball glass and mash with a teaspoon. Add crushed ice to fill the glass, then add the bourbon. Decorate with the other sprig of mint.

SAKETINI ‹

SERVES 1
3 measures gin
½ measure sake
twist of lemon peel

Vigorously shake the gin and sake over ice cubes until well frosted. Strain into a chilled cocktail glass and dress with a twist of lemon peel.

MANHATTAN DRY

This is a slightly sharper version of the classic Manhattan (page 171), using dry rather than sweet vermouth and curaçao.

SERVES 1
cracked ice
dash of Angostura bitters
3 measures rye whiskey
1 measure dry vermouth
2 dashes curaçao
cocktail cherry

Stir the liquids over cracked ice in a mixing glass and mix well. Strain into a chilled cocktail glass and decorate with a cocktail cherry.

There are a number of other versions of the Manhattan, including a Womanhattan, which comprises 1 measure of grenadine with 2 measures of rye whiskey, served with a twist of lemon peel.

PEACH DAIQUIRI ▲

SERVES 1
2 measures white rum
1 measure lime juice
½ tsp sugar syrup
½ peach, peeled, stoned and chopped

Blend the white rum, lime juice, sugar syrup and chopped peach until smooth, then pour, without straining, into a chilled wine glass or lowball glass.

STREGA SOUR

SERVES 1
2 measures gin
1 measure Strega
1 measure lemon juice
lemon slice

Pour the gin, Strega and lemon juice over ice cubes and shake vigorously until well frosted. Strain into a cocktail glass and decorate with a slice of lemon.

BOSTON SIDECAR

SERVES 1
1½ measures white rum
½ measure brandy
½ measure triple sec
½ measure lemon juice
twist of orange peel

Pour the white rum, brandy, triple sec and lemon juice over ice cubes and shake vigorously until well frosted. Strain into a chilled cocktail glass and decorate with a twist of orange peel.

RACQUET CLUB ◄

SERVES 1

dash of orange bitters

1 measure gin

1 measure dry vermouth

twist of orange peel

Dash the orange bitters over ice cubes in a mixing glass and pour in the gin and dry vermouth. Stir well to mix, then strain into a chilled cocktail glass. Serve with a twist of orange peel.

METROPOLITAN

SERVES 1

lemon wedge

1 tbsp caster sugar

cracked ice

½ measure vodka or lemon vodka

½ measure crème de framboise or other
   raspberry liqueur

½ measure cranberry juice

½ measure orange juice

2 cranberries

Rub the outside rim of a cocktail glass with the lemon and dip it into the sugar to frost. Set aside. Put the cracked ice into a cocktail shaker and pour in the vodka, liqueur, cranberry juice and orange juice. Shake vigorously for 10–20 seconds. Strain into the chilled glass, taking care not to disturb the frosting, and decorate with the cranberries.

SHADY LADY ▲

SERVES 1

3 measures tequila

1 measure apple brandy

1 measure cranberry juice

dash of lime juice

Shake the tequila, apple brandy, cranberry juice and a dash of lime juice over ice cubes until well frosted. Strain into a chilled cocktail glass.

MULE'S HIND LEG ▸

SERVES 1
½ measure apricot brandy
½ measure apple brandy
½ measure Benedictine
½ measure gin
½ measure maple syrup

Vigorously shake the apricot brandy, apple brandy, Benedictine, gin and maple syrup over ice cubes until well frosted. Strain into a chilled cocktail glass.

CHAMPAGNE COCKTAIL ▸

The classic champagne cocktail can be too sweet for some people, so you can leave the sugar out as it is the brandy that gives the treat and the kick.

SERVES 1
1 sugar cube
2 dashes of Angostura bitters
1 measure brandy
champagne, chilled

Place the sugar cube with the dashes of bitters in the base of a chilled flute. Pour on the brandy and top up slowly with champagne.

MOJITO

The rum in this cocktail, which was allegedly a favourite of writer Ernest Hemingway, is rich in flavour and redolent of holiday memories full of sunshine.

SERVES 1
1 tsp sugar
7 mint leaves
juice of half a lime
crushed ice
2 measures light rum
soda water

Put the sugar, six mint leaves and the lime juice in a highball glass and crush or muddle the mint. Add the crushed ice and rum, then top up with soda water. Finish with the remaining mint leaf.

PLANTER'S COCKTAIL ▲

SERVES 1
1 measure rum
juice of half a lime
1 tsp sugar syrup
dash of Angostura bitters

Mix the rum with the lime juice, sugar syrup and a dash of Angostura bitters. Serve in a cocktail glass or lowball glass.

DEAUVILLE PASSION

Deauville was elegant, extravagant and very fashionable resort on the Normandy coast during the 1920s and no doubt many great cocktails were created there.

SERVES 1
1¾ measures cognac
1¼ measures apricot curaçao
1¼ measures passion fruit juice
bitter lemon
mint leaves

Shake the cognac, apricot curaçao and passion fruit juice over ice cubes until well frosted. Strain into a chilled highball glass, top up with bitter lemon and dress with mint leaves.

LOUNGE LIZARD ◀

SERVES 1
cracked ice
2 measures dark rum
1 measure amaretto
cola

*Half fill a chilled highball glass with cracked ice and pour
the dark rum and amaretto over the ice. Top up with
cola and stir gently.*

PINK SHERBET ROYALE

This is perfect for very special occasions on hot days
or after dinner watching a warm sun setting slowly.

SERVES 2
300 ml/10 fl oz sparkling white wine, chilled
2 measures crème de cassis
1 measure brandy
1 scoop crushed ice
blackberries

*Whizz half the wine in a blender with the crème de cassis,
brandy and crushed ice until really frothy and frosted
(mind it doesn't bubble over). Slowly whisk in a little more
wine and pour into frosted highball glasses. Top with
a few blackberries.*

199

BLANCHE

SERVES 1

1 measure Pernod
1 measure triple sec
½ measure clear curaçao

Pour the Pernod, triple sec and clear curaçao over ice cubes and shake vigorously until well frosted. Strain into a chilled cocktail glass.

VODKATINI

A certain Mr Bond popularised the use of vodka, rather than gin, as the base for a Martini, hence the Vodkatini is now widely accepted as a stylish and delicious alternative.

SERVES 1

1 measure vodka
dash of dry vermouth
lemon peel or olive

Pour the vodka over a handful of ice cubes in a mixing glass. Add the vermouth, stir well and strain into a cocktail glass. Dress with lemon peel or an olive.

RAFFLES KNOCKOUT

SERVES 1

1 measure triple sec
1 measure kirsch
dash of lemon juice
cocktail cherries
lemon slice

Vigorously shake the triple sec, kirsch and lemon juice over ice cubes until well frosted. Strain into a chilled cocktail glass. Serve with some cocktail cherries and a lemon slice.

BIRD OF PARADISO ▾

SERVES 1
cracked ice
1½ measures white tequila
½ measure white crème de cacao
½ measure Galliano
1 measure orange juice
½ measure single cream
lemon wedges

Vigorously shake the white tequila, white crème de cacao, Galliano, orange juice and single cream over cracked ice until well frosted. Strain into a chilled wine glass. Serve with some lemon wedges on a cocktail stick.

DERBY DAIQUIRI ▸

SERVES 1
4–6 ice cubes
2 measures white rum
1 measure orange juice
½ measure triple sec
½ measure lime juice
twist of lime peel

Whizz the ice cubes, white rum, orange juice, triple sec and lime juice in a blender until smooth, then pour, without straining, into a chilled cocktail glass. Serve with a twist of lime peel.

FLIRTINI

This combination of vodka and champagne is guaranteed to bring a sparkle to the eyes and a smile to the lips – what could be more attractive?

SERVES 1
¼ slice fresh pineapple, chopped
½ measure Cointreau, chilled
½ measure vodka, chilled
1 measure pineapple juice, chilled
champagne or sparkling white wine, chilled

Put the pineapple and Cointreau into a mixing glass or jug and muddle with a spoon to crush the pineapple. Add the vodka and pineapple juice and stir well, then strain into a champagne flute. Top up with champagne, although sparkling white wine works well too.

The Mai Tai was created in 1944 by Californian restaurateur Victor Bergeron, known as Trader Vic, for friends visiting from Tahiti. On tasting the drink they allegedly cried out 'Mai Tai – Roe Ae,' meaning 'out of this world'.

MAI TAI

SERVES 1
cracked ice
2 measures white rum
2 measures dark rum
1 measure orange curaçao
1 measure lime juice
1 tbsp orgeat syrup
1 tbsp grenadine
cocktail cherries
pineapple slices
fruit peel

Shake the white and dark rums, curaçao, lime juice, orgeat syrup and grenadine vigorously over cracked ice until well frosted. Strain into a chilled cocktail glass and decorate flamboyantly with the cocktail cherries, pineapple slices and any other twists of fruit peel you have to hand.

DER RAUM

MELBOURNE

Some places are just ahead of the game and Melbourne's Der Raum is obviously one of them. The judges at the Australian Gourmet Traveller awards felt confident enough to name it 2008 Bar of the Year and *National Geographic* has also given it the nod as one of the world's best drinking establishments.

   Despite the German name (meaning 'the room'), this is no thigh-slapping Bavarian beerhall. Rather it's a dark bare-boards bar on a slightly scruffy Richmond street that takes drinking very seriously indeed. Der Raum isn't the first place to pride itself on its impeccable use of fresh fruit juices, although it hand-squeezes them daily. However, where else can boast of owning the world's

BEST FOR
serious drinking

PHARMACY

This is Matthew Bax's tribute to artist Damien Hirst.

SERVES 1

1 red pepper
1 pear, peeled and diced
40 ml/1½ fl oz Plymouth gin
½ lemon, chopped into pieces
20 ml/¾ fl oz honey water
  (10 ml/⅓ fl oz premium
  honey topped up with
  boiling bottled spring water)
large chunk of ice
10 ml/⅓ fl oz Aperol (Italian
  liqueur)
piece of sherbet or small
  sherbet sweet
large syringe
medical jar
steel medical tray

Roast the pepper over a flame. Wrap it in clingfilm, wait 15 minutes and then scrape off the skin. In a mixing glass, add the pepper and pear to the gin. Cover, refrigerate and leave to infuse for a few days. When you're ready to serve it, muddle the pieces of lemon in another mixing glass and then add the pepper, pear, gin and honey water. Shake with a large chunk of ice and strain into the frozen medical jar. Fill the syringe with the Aperol. To serve, place the medical jar, syringe and sherbet 'pill' on the medical tray. Before drinking, inject the Aperol into the drink and drop in the sherbet.

'What you think is your most original idea, you'll always find in some old book, where even if the recipe's not exact, someone's had the same thought processes.'

Owner, Matthew Bax

best cocktail ice-making machine, which produces 'the largest cube you've ever had the pleasure to drink with'? Apparently this cools your drink more slowly.

Der Raum is at the forefront of the new trend for 'molecular mixology'. This approach to cocktails is similar to the 'molecular gastronomy' practised by Heston Blumenthal at the Fat Duck in Bray and by studying the science of taste, Der Raum's owner and executive bartender Matthew Bax has certainly taken a leaf from the famous chef's book.

On Thursday nights, the bartenders run a 'test lab' where they experiment with new mixtures, but every evening customers are treated to a spectacular sight behind the bar, where hundreds of spirit bottles hang from the ceiling by elastic straps, like a dense, swaying forest, all within the staff's easy reach.

DER RAUM
438 Church Street
Richmond
3121 Melbourne
Victoria
Australia
+61 3 9428 0055
www.derraum.com.au

Open Tuesday to Saturday
5.30 p.m. to 1.00 a.m.

KEEPING A CLEAR HEAD

Maybe you're watching your alcohol intake or recovering from an earlier session. Perhaps you're the designated driver or not yet of legal drinking age. Either way, you'll find that this selection of non-alcoholic cocktails – or 'mocktails' – can be just as interesting and delicious as alcoholic ones.

SHIRLEY TEMPLE ◂

SERVES 1
2 measures lemon juice
½ measure grenadine
½ measure sugar syrup
cracked ice
ginger ale
orange slice

Pour the lemon juice, grenadine and sugar syrup over ice cubes and shake vigorously until well frosted. Half fill a small, chilled highball glass with cracked ice and strain the liquid into it. Top up with ginger ale and dress with a slice of orange.

With her blonde ringlets, tap-dancing prowess and affecting ability to portray orphans, in the 1930s Shirley Temple was an enormous box-office draw. However, when the pint-sized actress went to premieres and parties with adult movie stars she was unfortunately too young to have whatever it was they were having. As a consequence, a thoughtful bartender mixed the original kiddie cocktail especially for her.

When she grew up, and became Shirley Temple Black, she also became a respected US diplomat. When asked to comment on the drink, Temple allegedly said she doesn't like it, because it's too sweet and she has never made a cent out of the use of her name.

CITRUS FIZZ

This clever and refreshing variation on the classic Buck's Fizz is perfect for all the family.

SERVES 1

2 measures fresh orange juice, chilled

caster sugar

a squeeze of lime juice

a few drops of Angostura bitters

2–3 measures sparkling water, chilled

Dip the rim of a flute into the orange juice and then into the caster sugar. Stir together the rest of the orange juice, the lime juice and the bitters and then pour the liquid into the glass. Top up with water to taste.

TEXAS VIRGIN ▸

SERVES 1

1 measure lime juice

1 measure barbecue sauce

Worcestershire sauce

Tabasco sauce

tomato juice

lime slices

1 pickled jalapeño chilli

Shake the lime juice, barbecue sauce and dashes of Worcestershire and Tabasco sauce over ice cubes until well frosted. Pour into a chilled highball glass, top up with tomato juice and stir. Dress with a couple of slices of lime and a pickled jalapeño chilli.

BABY BELLINI ▸

SERVES 1

2 measures peach juice

1 measure lemon juice

sparkling apple juice

Pour the peach juice and lemon juice into a chilled champagne flute and stir well. Top up with sparkling apple juice and stir again.

BITE OF THE APPLE ▲

SERVES 1

crushed ice

5 measures apple juice

1 measure lime juice

½ tsp orgeat syrup

1 tbsp apple sauce or apple purée

cinnamon

Whizz the crushed ice in a blender with the apple juice, lime juice, orgeat syrup and apple sauce until smooth. Pour into a chilled lowball glass and sprinkle with cinnamon.

BRIGHT GREEN COOLER ▲

SERVES 1

3 measures pineapple juice

2 measures lime juice

1 measure green peppermint syrup

cracked ice

ginger ale

twist of cucumber

lime slice

Pour the pineapple juice, lime juice and green peppermint syrup over ice cubes and shake vigorously until well frosted. Half fill a tall chilled highball glass with the cracked ice and strain the cocktail over it. Top up with ginger ale and dress with cucumber and lime.

SANGRÍA SECA ‹

SERVES 6
475 ml / 16 fl oz tomato juice
250 ml / 8 fl oz orange juice
3 measures lime juice
½ measure Tabasco sauce
2 tsp Worcestershire sauce
1 jalapeño chilli, deseeded and finely chopped
celery salt
white pepper (preferably freshly ground)
cracked ice

Pour the tomato juice, orange juice, lime juice, Tabasco and Worcestershire sauce into a jug. Add the chopped chilli and season with the celery salt and white pepper. Stir well, cover and chill in the refrigerator for at least an hour. To serve, half fill chilled highball glasses with cracked ice and strain the cocktail over it.

Sangría Seca makes a perfect long, cold drink for a crowd of friends at a summer barbecue – but without the alcohol. It's great for drivers and for those who have to stand around while others get a little merry.

POM POM

In this thirst-quencher, lemonade is transformed into an extravaganza that's pretty and pink, with a frothy topping to match its frivolous name.

SERVES 1
juice of half a lemon
1 egg white
1 dash grenadine
crushed ice
lemonade
lemon slice

Shake the lemon juice, egg white and grenadine together over ice cubes and strain into a highball glass half filled with crushed ice. Top up with the lemonade and dress with a slice of lemon on the rim of the glass.

COCOBERRY

SERVES 1
90 g/3½ oz raspberries
crushed ice
1 measure coconut cream
150 ml/5 fl oz pineapple juice
pineapple wedge
a few raspberries

Rub the raspberries through a metal strainer with the back of a spoon and transfer the purée to a blender. Add the crushed ice, coconut cream and pineapple juice. Blend until smooth, then pour the mixture, without straining, into a chilled lowball glass or highball glass. Dress with a pineapple wedge and fresh raspberries.

MOCHA SLUSH

Definitely for people with a sweet tooth, this is a chocoholic's dream and is popular with adults as well as children.

SERVES 1
crushed ice
2 measures coffee syrup
1 measure chocolate syrup
4 measures milk
grated chocolate

In a small blender, whizz together the crushed ice, coffee syrup, chocolate syrup and milk until slushy. Pour into a chilled wine glass and sprinkle with grated chocolate.

SALTY PUPPY

SERVES 1
granulated sugar
coarse salt
wedge of lime
cracked ice
½ measure lime juice
grapefruit juice

Mix equal quantities of the sugar and salt together on a saucer. Rub the rim of a chilled highball glass with a wedge of lime and dip it into the sugar and salt mixture to frost it. Fill the glass with cracked ice and pour the lime juice over them. Top up with grapefruit juice.

MINI COLADA ▲

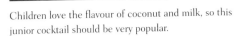

Children love the flavour of coconut and milk, so this junior cocktail should be very popular.

SERVES 2

6 measures cold milk
4 measures pineapple juice
3 measures coconut cream
pineapple cubes
pineapple leaves
a few cherries

Shake all the ingredients except the fruit together over ice cubes until well chilled. Pour into highball glasses with more ice cubes, finish each with pieces of pineapple, a pineapple leaf and a cherry on a stick, and drink through straws.

KNICKS VICTORY COOLER ▲

SERVES 1

cracked ice
2 measures apricot juice
raspberry juice
spiral of orange peel
a few raspberries

Half fill a chilled highball glass with the cracked ice. Pour the apricot juice over the ice, top up with raspberry juice and stir gently. Decorate with a spiral of orange peel and fresh raspberries.

PEACHY CREAM ◄

SERVES 1
2 measures peach juice, chilled
2 measures single cream
cracked ice

Pour the peach juice and cream together over ice cubes and shake vigorously until well frosted. Half fill a chilled highball glass or lowball glass with cracked ice and strain the cocktail over it.

CLAM DIGGER

SERVES 1
Tabasco sauce
Worcestershire sauce
¼ tsp horseradish sauce
4 measures tomato juice
4 measures clam juice
cracked ice
celery salt
black pepper, freshly ground
celery stick
lime wedge

Put ice cubes, sauces and juices into a cocktail shaker and shake vigorously. Fill a chilled highball glass with cracked ice and strain in the cocktail. Season with celery salt and pepper and dress with celery and lime.

The Clam Digger is a good cocktail for a Sunday brunch, when alcoholic drinks can be too soporific and you end up wasting the rest of the day, but you still want something to wake up the taste buds and set them tingling.

VIRGIN MARY

Simply a non-alcoholic Bloody Mary (page 98).

SERVES 1
cracked ice
3 measures tomato juice
1 measure lemon juice
2 dashes Worcestershire sauce
1 dash Tabasco sauce
celery salt
black pepper
lemon wedge
celery stick

Shake the tomato juice, lemon juice, Worcestershire sauce and Tabasco vigorously over the cracked ice and season with celery salt and black pepper. Strain into an iced old-fashioned or lowball glass and dress with lemon and celery.

GINGER FIZZ

This is a cool, refreshing cocktail for a hot day that is easiest made in a blender.

SERVES 1
ginger ale
8 fresh mint leaves
cracked ice
a few raspberries
mint sprig

Put the ginger ale and several mint leaves into a blender and whizz them together. Strain into a chilled highball glass two-thirds filled with cracked ice. Dress with the raspberries and a sprig of fresh mint.

SUNRISE ▲

SERVES 1
cracked ice
2 measures orange juice
1 measure lemon juice
1 measure grenadine
sparkling mineral water

Put the cracked ice into a chilled highball glass and pour the orange juice, lemon juice and grenadine over it. Stir together well and top up with sparkling mineral water.

PEACHY MELBA

SERVES 1
3 measures peach juice
1 measure lemon juice
1 measure lime juice
1 measure grenadine
peach slice

Shake the peach juice, lemon juice, lime juice and grenadine over ice cubes until well frosted. Strain into a chilled lowball glass and dress with a slice of peach.

PROHIBITION PUNCH ▲

SERVES 25
900 ml/1½ pints apple juice
350 ml/12 fl oz lemon juice
125 ml/4 fl oz sugar syrup
cracked ice
2¼ litres/4 pints ginger ale
orange slices

Pour the apple juice, lemon juice and sugar syrup into a large jug. Add the cracked ice and ginger ale. Stir gently to mix. Serve in chilled highball or lowball glasses with slices of orange and straws.

ITALIAN SODA

Italian syrup is available from most Italian delicatessens and supermarkets and comes in a wide variety of flavours, including a range of fruits and nuts, so you can substitute your favourite and vary the volume to taste.

SERVES 1
cracked ice
1½ measures Italian hazelnut syrup
sparkling water
lime slice

Fill a chilled highball glass with cracked ice. Pour the hazelnut syrup over and top up with sparkling water. Stir gently and dress with a slice of lime.

HEAVENLY DAYS ▲

SERVES 1
2 measures hazelnut syrup
2 measures lemon juice
1 tsp grenadine
cracked ice
sparkling water
lime slice
star fruit slice

Pour the hazelnut syrup, lemon juice and grenadine over ice cubes and shake vigorously until well frosted. Half fill a highball glass with the cracked ice and strain the cocktail over it. Top up with sparkling water. Stir gently and dress with slices of fruit.

COOL COLLINS ▶

SERVES 1
6 fresh mint leaves
1 tsp caster sugar
2 measures lemon juice
cracked ice
sparkling water
mint sprig
lemon slice

Put the mint leaves into a chilled highball glass and add the caster sugar and lemon juice. Crush the leaves with a spoon until the sugar has dissolved. Fill the glass with cracked ice and top up with sparkling water. Stir gently and decorate with a sprig of fresh mint and a slice of lemon.

BANANA COFFEE BREAK ◄

SERVES 2
300 ml/10 fl oz milk
4 tbsp instant coffee powder
150 g/5 oz vanilla ice cream
2 bananas, sliced and frozen
brown sugar to taste

Pour the milk into a food processor, add the coffee powder and process gently until combined. Add half the vanilla ice cream and process gently, then add the remaining ice cream and process until well combined. When the mixture is thoroughly blended, add the bananas and sugar to taste and process until smooth. Pour the mixture into highball or hurricane glasses and serve dressed with a few slices of banana.

ST CLEMENTS

SERVES 1
cracked ice
2 measures fresh orange juice
2 measures bitter lemon
orange slice
lemon slice

Put the cracked ice into a chilled highball glass. Pour in the orange juice and bitter lemon. Stir gently and dress with a slice of orange and a slice of lemon.

Thanks to the coffee, the Banana Coffee Break is a very adult-tasting, smoothie-style cocktail. In warm weather it makes an excellent mid-morning pick-me-up.

CALIFORNIA SMOOTHIE

The secret of a successful smoothie, whether alcoholic or non-alcoholic, is to blend the mixture at a medium speed until it is just smooth.

SERVES 1
1 banana, peeled and thinly sliced
60 g/2½ fl oz strawberries
90 g/3½ fl oz stoned dates
4½ tsp clear honey
250 ml/8 fl oz orange juice
4–6 ice cubes, crushed

Put the banana, strawberries, dates and honey into a blender and whizz until smooth. Add the orange juice and crushed ice and blend again until smooth. Pour into a chilled highball glass.

MOCHA CREAM

SERVES 2
200 ml/7 fl oz milk
50 ml/2 fl oz single cream
1 tbsp brown sugar
2 tbsp cocoa powder
1 tbsp coffee syrup
6 ice cubes
a little whipped cream
grated chocolate

Put the milk, cream and sugar into a food processor and process until combined. Add the cocoa powder and coffee syrup and process well. Then add the ice cubes and process until smooth. Pour the mixture into chilled highball glasses, and top with whipped cream and some grated chocolate.

Although the Mocha Cream recipe looks as though it will be very rich, filling and bad for the waistline, the resulting drink is actually quite light and delicate.

RED APPLE SUNSET ▲

SERVES 1
2 measures apple juice
2 measures grapefruit juice
dash of grenadine

Shake the apple juice, grapefruit juice and a dash of grenadine over ice cubes until well frosted. Strain into a chilled cocktail glass.

UNDER THE BOARDWALK ▸

SERVES 1
crushed ice
2 measures lemon juice
½ tsp sugar syrup
½ peach, peeled, stoned and chopped
sparkling water
a few raspberries

*Whizz the crushed ice in a blender with the lemon juice,
sugar syrup and peach until slushy. Pour into a chilled
highball glass or lowball glass. Top up with sparkling
water and stir gently. Dress with raspberries.*

COCONUT ISLANDER

SERVES 4
1 pineapple
4 measures pineapple juice
4 tbsp creamed coconut
4 measures milk
2 tbsp crushed pineapple
3 tbsp coconut flakes
crushed ice
cherries

*Cut the top off the pineapple and remove the flesh. Set
most of this aside for a dessert, but save a little of it to add
to the cocktail. Whizz all the ingredients except the cherries
in a blender with a little crushed ice for 30–40 seconds.
When smooth and frothy, pour into the pineapple shell,
dress with a few cherries and drink with straws.*

COCOBELLE

If you have a steady hand, this drink can be served
with pretty swirls of colour up the sides.

SERVES 1
3 measures cold milk
1 measure coconut cream
2 scoops vanilla ice cream
3–4 ice cubes
grenadine
toasted long-shred coconut or fresh coconut flakes

*Whizz the milk, coconut cream, ice cream and ice cubes
in a blender until slushy. Chill a highball glass and gently
dribble a few splashes of grenadine down the insides.
Pour the slush in slowly, so the colour doesn't all dissolve
at once, and sprinkle coconut on top.*

NEW ENGLAND PARTY ‹

SERVES 2
crushed ice
dash of Tabasco sauce
dash of Worcestershire sauce
1 tsp lemon juice
1 medium carrot, chopped
2 celery sticks, chopped
300 ml/10 fl oz tomato juice
150 ml/5 fl oz clam juice
salt
black pepper, freshly ground
celery stick, whole

Put all the ingredients, except the seasoning and celery stick into a blender and blend until smooth. Transfer to a jug, cover and chill for about an hour. Pour into two chilled highball glasses and season. Dress with a celery stick.

SLUSH PUPPY

Pink, pretty and refreshing – it looks serious, but you won't need to book a taxi home.

SERVES 1
juice of 1 lemon or ½ pink grapefruit
½ measure grenadine
a few strips of lemon peel
2–3 tsp raspberry syrup
soda water
1 maraschino cherry

Fill a highball glass with ice cubes and pour in the lemon juice and grenadine. Add the lemon peel, syrup and soda water to taste, and finish off with the cherry.

NON-ALCOHOLIC PIMM'S

SERVES 6
600 ml/1 pint lemonade, chilled
450 ml/15 fl oz cola, chilled
450 ml/15 fl oz dry ginger, chilled
juice of 1 orange
juice of 1 lemon
a few drops of Angostura bitters
fruit slices
mint sprigs

Mix the lemonade, cola, dry ginger, orange juice, lemon juice and bitters together in a large jug or punch bowl. Float in the fruit slices and mint, keep in a cold place and add ice cubes at the last minute. Serve in chilled highball glasses for a really cooling effect.

The joy of Non-Alcoholic Pimm's is that for occasions when you are drinking the real thing, drivers and the younger members of the family can also join in with no side-effects.

THAI FRUIT COCKTAIL

When choosing your favourite combination of juices, do make sure you use some of the more delicate oriental flavours.

SERVES 1

1 measure pineapple juice
1 measure orange juice
½ measure lime juice
1 measure passion fruit juice
2 measures guava juice
crushed ice
1 flower

Shake all the juices together with the crushed ice. Pour into a chilled highball glass and decorate with a flower.

FRUIT COOLER ▲

This is a great breakfast energiser and gives you a healthy start to the day, once you've done your workout.

SERVES 2

250 ml/8 fl oz orange juice
125 ml/4 fl oz natural yoghurt
2 eggs
2 bananas, sliced and frozen
fresh banana slices

Pour the orange juice and yoghurt into a food processor and process gently until combined. Add the eggs and frozen bananas and process until smooth. Pour the mixture into highball or hurricane glasses and decorate the rims with slices of fresh banana.

APPLE FRAZZLE

SERVES 1

4 measures apple juice

1 tsp sugar syrup

½ tsp lemon juice

sparkling mineral water

Pour the apple juice, sugar syrup and lemon juice over ice cubes and shake vigorously until well frosted. Strain into a chilled highball glass and top up with sparkling mineral water.

SOBER SUNDAY

An interesting variation for those who aren't drinking and anyone who is driving.

SERVES 1

cracked ice

1 measure grenadine

1 measure fresh lemon or lime juice

lemonade

lemon slices

lime slices

Pour the grenadine and fruit juice into a highball glass filled with cracked ice. Top up with lemonade and finish with lemon and lime slices.

FAUX KIR ROYALE ▲

SERVES 1

4–6 ice cubes, cracked

1½ measures raspberry syrup

sparkling apple juice, chilled

Put the cracked ice into a mixing glass and pour the raspberry syrup over it. Stir well to mix, then strain into a wine glass. Top up with chilled sparkling apple juice and stir.

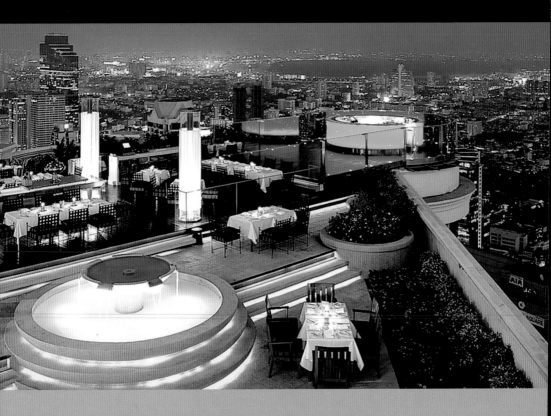

SKY BAR AT SIROCCO

BANGKOK

Sixty-three floors and 247m up, yet still out in the open, the Sky Bar at Sirocco has been known to make the most hardened of travel writers gasp. Literally the world's most breathtaking watering hole, it has those who thought themselves totally impervious to vertigo at least thinking about it. Even without the hip crowd of local glitterati, no other bar has quite the same wow factor as this.

To arrive in this dramatic location, you take the lift to the 64th floor 'dome' of the State Tower, where an open-sided staircase descends one floor to an uncovered deck (closed in inclement weather). On one side is a restaurant. On the other, the oval-shaped Sky Bar is cantilevered over the edge of the building, seeming to

BEST FOR

wow factor

SKY BAR COSMOPOLITAN

SERVES 1

30 ml/1 fl oz vodka
3 tsp Grand Marnier
1½ tsp crème de cassis
1½ tsp lime juice
30 ml/1 fl oz cranberry juice
orange peel

Shake the vodka, Grand Marnier, crème de cassis, lime juice and cranberry juice vigorously in a shaker with ice cubes for ten seconds. Strain into a frosted Martini glass and garnish with the orange peel.

❖

'Sirocco's Sky Bar is one of the world's highest al fresco bars so, as you can imagine, it has simply the most overwhelming views of Bangkok.'

Senior restaurant manager
Siriluk Pukalanont

defy gravity. A chest-high Plexiglass barrier is all that separates imbibers from the precipice.

Peering down from Bangkok's second-tallest skyscraper the cars below look like ants and the Chao Phraya River a trickle. Previous guests have commented that the aeroplanes overhead seem just as close as the ground below. To add to the atmosphere, a jazz band plays and the illuminated bar is multi-hued, glowing blue, pink and green, and changing colour every few minutes.

Given everything else going on, what's most surprising is that the cocktails here are no afterthought. If you can take your eyes off the view, you'll notice there's an extensive cocktail menu using top-quality spirits. Sky Bar's cocktails are renowned for their strength, but for those who prefer to stay 100 per cent sober in this environment, non-alcoholic drinks are also on the list.

SKY BAR AT SIROCCO
The Dome at State Tower
1055 Silom Rd
Bangrak
Bangkok 10500
+66 2 624 9555
www.thedomebkk.com

Open daily
6.00 p.m.–1.00 a.m.

AFTER DINNER

A good cocktail can be the perfect way to finish off a meal. You may forgo dessert and opt for a fruity, creamy cocktail or you may choose something more astringent to aid digestion and set you up for another drink. Either way, one of these specially selected recipes is bound to suit.

POUSSE-CAFÉ ‹

A pousse-café is a layered cocktail of many different coloured liqueurs. Each liqueur has a different density, so that when it's floated on top of the previous one it maintains its relative position in the glass.

SERVES 1
¼ measure grenadine
¼ measure crème de menthe
¼ measure Galliano
¼ measure kümmel
¼ measure brandy

Chill the grenadine, crème de menthe, Galliano, kümmel and brandy.

Pour the grenadine into a chilled shot or pousse-café glass. Then carefully trickle the crème de menthe over the back of a spoon evenly over the grenadine. Repeat with the Galliano, kümmel and brandy – in that order.

Well, enough of the theory. In practice it takes a certain amount of experience to gently but steadily pour the liqueurs over the back of a spoon. However, it's a skill that can be mastered.

Here are a couple of useful tips for making a Pousse-café. Firstly, it is crucial to thoroughly chill all the liqueurs first and, secondly, do add the liqueurs in the order listed in the recipe. If you don't do these things, the cocktail will still taste delicious, but you could end up with a rather unsightly mess, which is definitely not the point of a Pousse-café.

SAVOY SANGAREE

Port is a well known after-dinner drink. Here it is incorporated into a sophisticated cocktail.

SERVES 1
6 ice cubes, cracked
1 measure port
1 tsp caster sugar
freshly grated nutmeg

Put the cracked ice into a mixing glass, pour in the port and caster sugar, and stir until dissolved. Strain into a chilled cocktail glass or lowball glass and sprinkle with freshly grated nutmeg.

VODKA ESPRESSO

This makes a fabulous after-dinner treat. It's usually made with Stolichnaya vodka and Amarula, a South African cream liqueur with a caramel flavour.

SERVES 1
cracked ice
2 measures espresso or other strong brewed
    coffee, cooled
1 measure vodka
2 tsp caster sugar
1 measure Amarula

Put the cracked ice into a cocktail shaker, pour in the coffee, vodka and sugar. Cover and shake vigorously for 10-20 seconds, until the outside of the shaker is misted. Strain into a cocktail glass, then float the Amarula on top.

STARS AND STRIPES

SERVES 1
¾ measure cherry brandy, chilled
1½ measures single cream, chilled
¾ measure blue curaçao, chilled

Pour the chilled cherry brandy into a chilled shot glass or pousse-café glass. With a steady hand, gently pour in the chilled single cream using the back of a teaspoon to make a second layer and, finally, gently pour in the blue curaçao in the same way.

FANCY FREE

The key to this layered drink is to chill the liqueur and the glass in the freezer. If it does seem to mix on impact, give it a little time to settle and form its layers again.

SERVES 1

⅓ measure cherry brandy, iced
⅓ measure Cointreau, iced
⅓ measure apricot liqueur, iced

Into a chilled pousse-café or wine glass pour the cherry brandy. Then trickle in the Cointreau over the back of a spoon and repeat with the apricot liqueur.

GODDAUGHTER ▲

SERVES 1

4–6 ice cubes, crushed
2 measures apple brandy
1 measure amaretto
1 tbsp apple sauce
ground cinnamon

Put the crushed ice into a blender and add the apple brandy, amaretto and apple sauce. Blend until smooth, then pour the mixture, without straining, into a chilled wine glass. Sprinkle with ground cinnamon and serve.

GODSON

SERVES 1
4–6 ice cubes, cracked
2 measures amaretto
orange juice
orange slice

Put the cracked ice into a chilled highball glass. Pour in the amaretto and top up with the orange juice. Stir well to mix and decorate with a slice of orange.

GOLDEN CADILLAC

SERVES 1
1 measure triple sec
1 measure Galliano
1 measure single cream

Pour the triple sec, Galliano and single cream over ice cubes and shake vigorously until well frosted. Strain the mixture into a chilled cocktail glass.

OLD PAL ‣

SERVES 1
2 measures rye whiskey
1½ measures Campari
1 measure sweet vermouth

Pour the rye whiskey, Campari and sweet vermouth over ice cubes in a shaker and shake vigorously until well frosted. Strain into a chilled cocktail glass.

Why the name Mary is so closely associated with cocktails is a mystery. Bloody Mary was, of course, Mary Tudor (1516–58); while the MQS was named after Mary Queen of Scots (1542–67). Be careful to strain this pleasingly strong mixture well, as it will spoil if watered down.

MQS ‣

SERVES 1
lemon wedge
caster sugar
4–6 ice cubes, cracked
2 measures Scotch whisky
1 measure Drambuie
1 measure green Chartreuse

Rub the rim of a chilled cocktail glass with a wedge of lemon, then dip the glass into the caster sugar to frost it. Put the cracked ice into a mixing glass and pour in the Scotch whisky, Drambuie and green Chartreuse. Stir to mix and strain into the prepared glass.

TRICOLOR ‹

SERVES 1

1 measure crème de menthe, chilled
1 measure Baileys Irish Cream, chilled
1 measure red maraschino, chilled

Pour the chilled crème de menthe into a chilled shot glass. With a steady hand, gently pour in the chilled Baileys Irish Cream down the back of a teaspoon to make a second layer and, for the final layer, repeat with the chilled red maraschino.

BLACK WIDOW

Not as wicked as its title suggests, but if you're feeling adventurous you could take it straight, on the rocks.

SERVES 1

⅔ measure dark rum
⅓ measure Southern Comfort
juice of half a lime
dash of curaçao
soda water
lime peel

Pour the dark rum, Southern Comfort, lime juice and a dash of curaçao over ice cubes and shake together well and strain into a chilled highball glass. Top up with soda water and finish with a twist of lime.

ELK'S OWN ▲

SERVES 1

2 measures rye whiskey
1 measure ruby port
½ measure lemon juice
1 tsp sugar syrup
1 egg white
star fruit slices

Pour the rye whiskey, ruby port, lemon juice, sugar syrup and egg white over ice cubes and shake vigorously until well frosted. Strain into a chilled cocktail glass and dress with star fruit slices.

BACCARAT ▶

Cocktails have always been enjoyed at casinos and go hand in hand with the atmosphere of risk and gamble.

SERVES 1
1 measure Jack Daniel's
½ measure Dubonnet
2 dashes of crème de cassis

Pour the Jack Daniel's, Dubonnet and crème de cassis over ice cubes and shake together well until frosted. Strain into a chilled cocktail glass.

GODMOTHER ▲

SERVES 1
4–6 ice cubes, cracked
2 measures vodka
1 measure amaretto

Put the cracked ice into a chilled highball glass and pour the vodka and amaretto over it. Stir to mix.

Unsurprisingly, the recipe for the Godmother is a variant on the popular 1970s cocktail the Godfather, which also contains the Italian liqueur amaretto.

CHERRYCOLA ▲

SERVES 1
6–8 ice cubes, cracked
2 measures cherry brandy
1 measure lemon juice
cola
lemon slice

*Half fill a chilled highball glass or lowball glass with the
cracked ice. Pour the cherry brandy and lemon juice
over the ice. Top up with cola, stir gently and decorate
with a slice of lemon.*

GODCHILD ▲

SERVES 1
4–6 ice cubes, crushed
1½ measures amaretto
1 measure vodka
1 measure single cream

*Whizz the crushed ice in a blender with the amaretto,
vodka and single cream. Blend until smooth, then pour
into a chilled champagne flute.*

B52

In this recipe, Kahlúa can easily be substituted for the dark crème de cacao.

SERVES 1

1 measure dark crème de cacao, chilled
1 measure Baileys Irish Cream, chilled
1 measure Grand Marnier, chilled

Pour the chilled dark crème de cacao into a shot glass or pousse-café glass. With a steady hand, gently pour in the chilled Baileys Irish Cream to make a second layer, then gently pour in the chilled Grand Marnier.

BEADLESTONE ▲

SERVES 1

4–6 ice cubes, cracked
2 measures Scotch whisky
1½ measures dry vermouth

Put the cracked ice into a mixing glass and pour over the Scotch whisky and dry vermouth. Stir well to mix and strain into a chilled cocktail glass.

INDIAN SUMMER

The coffee liqueur is the key ingredient in this delicious long mix – it would be good with crème de noyau or crème de cacao too.

SERVES 1

1 measure vodka
2 measures Kahlúa
1 measure gin
2 measures pineapple
tonic water
lime slice
cucumber slice

Pour the vodka, Kahlúa, gin and pineapple juice over ice cubes and shake together well until frosted. Strain into a cocktail glass or wine glass and top up with the tonic water. Dress with lime and cucumber slices.

AVALANCHE

This rich combination of almonds from the amaretto, apricots from the brandy and juice is delicious after dinner, but you might want to pass on pudding.

SERVES 1

1 measure amaretto
½ measure apricot brandy
1 measure apricot or mango juice
1 scoop vanilla ice cream

Whizz the Amaretto, apricot brandy, apricot or mango juice and ice cream in a blender until well frosted and frothy. Pour into an iced cocktail glass and drink through a straw.

COWBOY

In movies, cowboys drink their rye straight, often pulling the cork out of the bottle with their teeth, and it is certainly difficult to imagine John Wayne or Clint Eastwood sipping delicately from a chilled cocktail glass, so use a lowball glass.

SERVES 1

3 measures rye whiskey
2 tbsp single cream

Pour the whiskey and cream over ice cubes and shake vigorously until well frosted. Strain into a chilled lowball glass.

OSBORNE

This cocktail was named after Queen Victoria's Isle of Wight residence and was, apparently, a favourite tipple of Her Majesty.

SERVES 1

3 measures claret
1 measure Scotch whisky

Pour the claret and Scotch whisky into a wine glass, stir and serve.

JEALOUSY

If you want a change, you could occasionally flavour the cream in this excellent after-dinner cocktail with a different liqueur.

SERVES 1
1 tsp crème de menthe
1–2 tbsp double cream
2 measures coffee or chocolate liqueur
chocolate matchsticks

Gently beat the crème de menthe into the cream until thick. Pour the coffee liqueur into a small iced cocktail glass and carefully spoon on the whipped flavoured cream. Serve with chocolate matchsticks.

WHISKEY SOUR

This drink originates in the American south and traditionally uses the best American whiskey, but it can also be made with vodka, gin or other spirits.

SERVES 1
1 measure lemon or lime juice
2 measures blended whiskey
1 tsp caster sugar or syrup de gomme
lemon or lime slice
maraschino cherry

Pour lemon juice, blended whiskey and caster sugar over ice cubes and shake and strain into a sour glass. Finish with a slice of lemon and a cherry.

MUDSLIDE

Despite its ominous-sounding name, this is a richly-flavoured creamy concoction that is beautiful whatever the weather.

SERVES 1
1½ measures Kahlúa
1½ measures Baileys Irish Cream
1½ measures vodka

Shake the Kahlúa, Baileys Irish Cream and vodka vigorously over ice cubes until well frosted. Strain into a chilled wine glass.

BLACK BUSH

Bourbon whiskey has its own distinctive flavour, which is warm, rich, oakey and brought out well here by the sloe gin.

SERVES 1
½ measure bourbon whiskey
½ measure sloe gin
4–6 ice cubes, cracked
fresh cherry

Stir the bourbon and sloe gin together with the cracked ice. Strain into a chilled cocktail glass and dress with a fresh cherry.

AMARETTO STINGER ◀

SERVES 1

2 measures amaretto

1 measure white crème de menthe

Pour the amaretto and white crème de menthe over ice cubes. Shake vigorously until well frosted and strain into a chilled cocktail glass or lowball glass.

GENOESE ◀

SERVES 1

1 measure vodka

1 measure grappa

½ measure Sambuca

½ measure dry vermouth

Vigorously shake the vodka, grappa, Sambuca and dry vermouth over ice cubes until well frosted. Strain into a chilled cocktail glass.

RASPBERRY LIFT-OFF ▶

If you're in need of a boost after a heavy meal, the fruity flavours and fizz of this cocktail will provide it, but for maximum lift make it with fresh juice and fruit, and the champagne must be freshly popped and bubbly.

SERVES 1
1 measure raspberry vodka
1 measure fresh raspberry juice
1 measure orange juice
champagne, chilled
raspberries

Pour the vodka, raspberry juice and orange juice over ice cubes and shake vigorously until well frosted. Strain into a chilled flute and top up with chilled champagne. Stir gently to mix and dress with raspberries.

WHISKEY SANGAREE ▲

SERVES 1
6 ice cubes, cracked
2 measures bourbon
1 tsp sugar syrup
soda water
1 tbsp ruby port
freshly grated nutmeg

Put the cracked ice into a chilled lowball glass. Pour on the bourbon and sugar syrup, and top up with soda water. Stir gently to mix, then float the ruby port on top. Sprinkle with freshly grated nutmeg.

ASHLEY WILKES ◂

Ashley Wilkes, of course, is the object of Scarlett O'Hara's obsession in *Gone With The Wind* and this recipe certainly has the feel of the American south.

SERVES 1
4 sprigs of fresh mint
1 tsp sugar
dash of lime juice
6 ice cubes, cracked
2 measures bourbon
1 measure peach brandy
sprig of mint

Crush three of the sprigs of mint and place them in a chilled highball glass. Add the sugar, lime juice and cracked ice. Pour in the bourbon and peach brandy, and stir to mix. Dress with the remaining sprig of mint.

TOFFEE SPLIT

You're unlikely to need a dessert as well, but you could always pour this over some ice cream.

SERVES 1
crushed ice
2 measures Drambuie
1 measure toffee liqueur, iced

Fill a shot glass with crushed ice. Pour in the Drambuie and then pour on the toffee liqueur, carefully from the side of the glass, so it layers on top. Drink immediately.

KENTUCKY ORANGE BLOSSOM ▸

SERVES 1
2 measures bourbon
1 measure orange juice
½ measure triple sec
orange wedge

Pour the bourbon, orange juice and triple sec over ice cubes and shake vigorously until well frosted. Strain into a chilled cocktail glass and dress with a wedge of orange.

OLD ETONIAN

SERVES 1
6–8 ice cubes, cracked
dash of crème de noyau
dash of orange bitters
1 measure gin
1 measure Lillet
orange peel

Put the cracked ice into a mixing glass and add the dashes of crème de noyau and orange bitters, and the gin and Lillet. Stir well to mix, then strain into a chilled cocktail glass. Squeeze over a piece of orange peel.

THISTLE

SERVES 1
4–6 ice cubes, cracked
dash of Angostura bitters
2 measures Scotch whisky
1½ measures sweet vermouth

Put the cracked ice into a mixing glass. Dash Angostura bitters over the ice and pour in the Scotch whisky and sweet vermouth. Stir well to mix and strain into a chilled cocktail glass.

GREAT DANE

SERVES 1
2 measures gin
1 measure cherry brandy
½ measure dry vermouth
1 tsp kirsch
twists of lemon peel

Pour the gin, cherry brandy, dry vermouth and kirsch over ice cubes and shake vigorously until well frosted. Strain into a chilled cocktail glass or highball glass and dress with twists of lemon peel.

BLACK RUSSIAN

History records only White and Red Russians. The omission of the Black Russian is a sad oversight. For the coffee liqueur, you can use either Tia Maria or Kahlúa, depending on your personal taste. The latter is sweeter.

SERVES 1
4–6 ice cubes, cracked
2 measures vodka
1 measure coffee liqueur

Pour the vodka and liqueur over the cracked ice in a chilled lowball glass. Stir to mix.

To create a White Russian, follow the Black Russian recipe and then float a tablespoon or so of thick cream on top. If you blend the ingredients instead, it becomes a Russian Coffee. For a Red Russian, substitute cherry brandy for the coffee liqueur, but don't add cream.

LONG GONE ▸

SERVES 1

2 measures bourbon

1 measure Drambuie

1 measure orange juice

dash of orange bitters

orange wedge

Pour the bourbon, Drambuie, orange juice and dash of orange bitters over ice cubes and shake vigorously until well frosted. Strain into a chilled cocktail glass. Dress with a wedge of orange.

FIFTH AVENUE

After-dinner cocktails often include cream and this one also has the delicate flavours of apricot and cocoa.

SERVES 1

1 measure dark crème de cacao, iced

1 measure apricot brandy, iced

1 measure cream

Pour the crème de cacao into a chilled cocktail glass. Carefully add a layer of apricot brandy over the back of a spoon resting against the edge of the glass. Repeat with a layer of cream. Each layer should float on top of the previous one.

CHOCOLATE STINGER ▸

A Stinger always contains crème de menthe and the drink arose in the days of Prohibition in the USA, with the sweet, minty liqueur being used to mask the flavour of the poor quality brandy available at the time.

SERVES 1

1 measure dark crème de cacao

1 measure white crème de menthe

Pour the dark crème de cacao and white crème de menthe over ice cubes. Shake vigorously until well frosted. Strain into a chilled cocktail glass or lowball glass.

LE BAR, HOTEL GEORGE V

PARIS

Opened in 1928, with a glitzy cocktail party to celebrate the launch of a transatlantic liner, the award-winning George V hotel has an illustrious history. There are plenty of trendy see-and-be-seen drinking spots in the French capital today. However, this Le Bar (there are others similarly named) constantly wins plaudits for being a Belle Epoque oasis in a bustling contemporary city.

The bar staff also get a special mention for being not only impeccably professional, but also courteous and friendly, without the slightest whiff of Parisian *hauteur*. Both the high-society dames and wealthy financiers who come regularly for aperitifs, and those for whom a visit is a special event, are treated like royalty (remember to dress relatively smartly).

BEST FOR
timeless elegance

TIME WAITS FOR NO ONE

While Le Bar is famous for its selection of Martinis, it has also recently created a menu using some of the world's oldest brandies, cognacs, whiskies and other spirits.

SERVES 1
cracked ice
120 ml/4 fl oz dark rum
2 tsp honey
1 cinnamon stick

Fill a cocktail glass with cracked ice and leave so that the ice chills the glass. Pour the dark rum and honey into a cocktail shaker and shake. Pour the mixture over the ice and stir with the cinnamon stick. Garnish with the cinnamon stick.

❖

'Le Bar has a very nice mix of Parisians and international guests from the hotel, not to mention some celebrities. This great crowd makes it typically Parisian – convivial and warm.'

Head barman: Johann Burgos

The room itself is cosily lined with mahogany and what is aptly described as 'cognac-coloured' wood. As guests lounge in sumptuous leather sofas, they can also gaze through the large plate-glass window out on to Avenue George V beyond.

Some older customers fondly remember the barmen who issued 'international mixing passports' and made the place even more legendary in the 1950s and 1960s. However, today's staff are upholding the standard with their Champagne Specials and stylishly presented fruit Martinis (sour apple and lychee are just two noteworthy flavours).

The hotel, which has been home to numerous world statesmen, was faithfully renovated by Four Seasons in the late 1990s, but its charming olde worlde bar has always been a refined reminder of the heyday of the cocktail era.

LE BAR
FOUR SEASONS HOTEL GEORGE V
31 Avenue George V
(near Rue Pierre Charron)
75008 Paris
+33 1 49 52 70 00
www.fourseasons.com/paris

Open
Sunday to Friday 10.00 a.m.–1.00 a.m.
Saturday 10.00 a.m.–2.00 a.m.
(3.00 p.m.–6.00 p.m. cocktails
6.00 p.m.–12.00 a.m. light entrées)

NIGHT OUT

Whether or not the point is to consume as much alcohol as possible, enjoying a cocktail or two with friends is an immensely pleasurable experience. If you intend to spend the evening in a bar, why not ask the bartender to mix one or more of these beauties for you?

TEQUILA SLAMMER ‹

Slammers are also known as shooters. The idea is that you pour the ingredients directly into the glass, without stirring. Cover the glass with one hand to prevent spillage, slam it on to a table to mix and down the cocktail in one. Do ensure you use a strong glass.

SERVES 1
1 measure white tequila, chilled
1 measure lemon juice
sparkling wine, chilled

Put the tequila and lemon juice into a chilled shot glass. Top up with sparkling wine. Cover the glass with your hand and slam on the table.

Unsurprisingly, this cocktail gets its name from the way it is commonly consumed. The slamming action releases bubbles of carbon dioxide, causing the drink to foam rather vigorously. It must be downed in one otherwise the bubbles will escape.

If you try this at home, you can substitute lemonade or ginger ale for the sparkling wine. You can also use real champagne, in which case the drink becomes a Slammer Royale.

Drinking slammers, or shooters, can mean that the drinker becomes intoxicated quickly; this is often exacerbated in a group situation where there can be a competitive element to drinking them.

ALABAMA SLAMMER

Small, but perfectly proportioned – this is a shooter with a real kick.

SERVES 1
cracked ice
1 measure Southern Comfort
1 measure amaretto
1 measure sloe gin
½ tsp lemon juice

Pour the Southern Comfort, amaretto and sloe gin over cracked ice in a mixing glass and stir. Strain into a shot glass and add the lemon juice. Cover with your hand and slam on the table.

ANKLE BREAKER ▲

SERVES 1
2 measures dark rum
1 measure cherry brandy
1 measure lime juice
1 tsp sugar syrup

Shake the dark rum, cherry brandy, lime juice and sugar syrup over ice cubes until well frosted. Strain into a chilled highball or lowball glass.

STAR WARS ▶

'A long time ago in a galaxy far, far away...' this cocktail was invented – or maybe not.

SERVES 1
2 measures gin
2 measures lemon juice
1 measure Galliano
1 measure crème de noyau
twist of lemon peel

Pour the gin, lemon juice, Galliano and crème de noyau over ice cubes and shake vigorously until well frosted. Strain into a chilled cocktail glass and serve with a twist of lemon peel.

HUATUSCO WHAMMER ‹

SERVES 1
1 measure white tequila
½ measure white rum
½ measure vodka
½ measure gin
½ measure triple sec
1 measure lemon juice
½ tsp sugar syrup
cracked ice
cola

Pour the tequila, rum, vodka, gin, triple sec, lemon juice and sugar syrup over ice cubes and shake vigorously until well frosted. Fill a chilled highball glass with cracked ice and strain the cocktail over it. Top up with cola, stir gently and serve with straws.

JOHN WOOD ▾

SERVES 1
cracked ice
2 measures sweet vermouth
½ measure kümmel
½ measure Irish whiskey
1 measure lemon juice
dash of Angostura bitters

Pour the vermouth, kümmel, whiskey and lemon juice over the cracked ice with a dash of Angostura bitters and shake vigorously until well frosted. Strain into a chilled wine glass.

Vermouth is an immensely useful cocktail flavouring as it contains more than 50 herbs and spices, and combines well with many spirits. It had fallen in popularity as a base for cocktails, but is now enjoying a revival.

CHESHIRE CAT ▸

This delicious concoction is sure to leave you grinning like the famous fictional feline character.

SERVES 1
cracked ice
1 measure brandy
1 measure sweet vermouth
1 measure orange juice
champagne, chilled
orange peel

Pour the brandy, sweet vermouth and orange juice over cracked ice in a mixing glass. Stir well, then strain into a chilled flute and top up with chilled champagne. Squeeze over a twist of orange peel.

CHERRY KITSCH

This is a velvety smooth cocktail, fruity but with a rich brandy undertone. A touch of maraschino liqueur added at the end would be good too.

SERVES 1
1 scoop crushed ice
1 measure cherry brandy
2 measures pineapple juice
½ measure kirsch
1 egg white
frozen maraschino cherry

Pour the cherry brandy, pineapple juice, kirsch and egg white over the crushed ice and shake well until frosted. Pour into a chilled highball glass and decorate with a frozen maraschino cherry.

MAGNOLIA BLOSSOM ▸

SERVES 1
2 measures gin
1 measure lemon juice
1 measure single cream

Pour the gin, lemon juice and single cream over ice cubes and shake vigorously until well frosted. Strain into a chilled cocktail glass.

CONEY ISLAND BABY

SERVES 1

2 measures peppermint schnapps
1 measure dark crème de cacao
cracked ice
soda water

Pour the peppermint schnapps and dark crème de cacao over ice cubes and shake vigorously until well frosted. Fill a chilled lowball glass with cracked ice and strain the cocktail over it. Top up with soda water.

UNION JACK

SERVES 1

1 measure maraschino, chilled
1 measure blue curaçao, chilled
1 measure grenadine, chilled

Pour the chilled maraschino into a chilled shot glass. With a steady hand, gently pour in the chilled blue curaçao to make a second layer and, finally, gently pour in the chilled grenadine.

VOODOO

This enthralling mixture of flavours is guaranteed to weave a spell on your taste buds and work its magic from the very first sip.

SERVES 1

½ measure Kahlúa, chilled
½ measure Malibu, chilled
½ measure butterscotch schnapps, chilled
1 measure milk, chilled

Pour the Kahlúa, Malibu, schnapps and milk into a highball glass and stir well.

FLYING SCOTSMAN ▲   🖫

SERVES 1

4–6 ice cubes, crushed

dash of Angostura bitters

2 measures Scotch whisky

1 measure sweet vermouth

¼ tsp sugar syrup

*Put the crushed ice into a blender, dash the Angostura
bitters over it and add the Scotch whisky, sweet vermouth
and sugar syrup. Blend until slushy and pour into a
chilled lowball glass.*

BANANA SLIP ▲   🖫

SERVES 1

1 measure crème de banane, chilled

1 measure Baileys Irish Cream, chilled

*Pour the chilled crème de banane into a shot glass. With
a steady hand, gently pour in the chilled Baileys Irish
Cream to make a second layer.*

AURORA BOREALIS ◂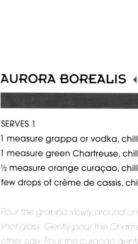

SERVES 1

1 measure grappa or vodka, chilled
1 measure green Chartreuse, chilled
½ measure orange curaçao, chilled
few drops of crème de cassis, chilled

*Pour the grappa slowly around one side of a well-chilled
shot glass. Gently pour the Chartreuse round the
other side. Pour the curaçao gently into the middle
and add a few drops of crème de cassis just before
serving. Don't stir. Drink slowly.*

FRENCH KISS

SERVES 1

2 measures bourbon
1 measure apricot liqueur
2 tsp grenadine
1 tsp lemon juice

*Pour the bourbon, apricot liqueur, grenadine and lemon
juice over ice cubes and shake vigorously until well
frosted. Strain into a chilled cocktail glass.*

The spectacular Aurora Borealis should not be mixed or stirred. Leave it to swirl around the glass, creating a multi-hued effect, and try to guess what the various flavours are.

FIREMAN'S SOUR ▸

SERVES 1

2 measures white rum

1½ measures lime juice

1 tbsp grenadine

1 tsp syrup de gomme

cocktail cherry

Shake the white rum, lime juice, grenadine and syrup de gomme over ice cubes until well frosted. Strain into a cocktail glass and decorate with a cocktail cherry.

BROADWAY SMILE ▴

SERVES 1

1 measure triple sec, chilled

1 measure crème de cassis, chilled

1 measure Swedish Punsch, chilled

Pour the triple sec into a chilled lowball glass. With a steady hand, pour the chilled crème de cassis on top, without mixing, and then pour the chilled Swedish Punsch on top, again without mixing.

FLYING GRASSHOPPER

There are two versions of this cocktail – one made with equal quantities of white and green crème de menthe and one with green crème de menthe and chocolate liqueur.

SERVES 1

cracked ice

1 measure vodka

1 measure green crème de menthe

1 measure white crème de menthe

Put the cracked ice into a mixing glass or jug and pour in the vodka and both types of crème de menthe. Stir well and strain into a highball glass.

PLANTATION PUNCH ◂

SERVES 1

2 measures dark rum

1 measure Southern Comfort

1 measure lemon juice

1 tsp brown sugar

sparkling water

1 tsp of ruby port

lemon slice

orange slice

Pour the dark rum, Southern Comfort, lemon juice and brown sugar over ice cubes and shake vigorously until well frosted. Strain into a chilled highball glass and top up, almost to the rim, with sparkling water. Float the ruby port on top by pouring it gently over the back of a teaspoon and garnish with slices of lemon and orange.

CUBAN ◂

SERVES 1

2 measures brandy

1 measure apricot brandy

1 measure lime juice

1 tsp white rum

Pour the brandy, apricot brandy, lime juice and white rum over ice cubes and shake vigorously until well frosted. Strain into a chilled cocktail glass.

ARCHIPELAGO

In this cocktail a colourful selection of flavours and fruits from many places is topped with a layer of cream, almost like fruit salad and cream in a bowl.

SERVES 1

1¼ measures cognac

¾ measure kiwi fruit juice or syrup

¼ measure mandarin liqueur

¼ measure chocolate liqueur

1 tbsp single cream

kiwi fruit slice or mint leaf

Stir the cognac, kiwi juice, mandarin liqueur and chocolate liqueur together over ice cubes in a chilled mixing glass and strain into a cocktail glass. Carefully pour the cream in a layer over the top. Dress with a kiwi fruit slice.

MRS FITZHERBERT ▾

This cocktail is named after Mrs Fitzherbert, who secretly married the Prince of Wales, later George IV. However, as she was a widow, a Catholic and the then king hadn't blessed the union, the prince was forced to divorce her and marry a wealthy Protestant princess instead. However, rumour has it that when he died he had a miniature of Mrs Fitzherbert around his neck.

SERVES 1
1 measure white port
1 measure cherry brandy

Pour the white port and cherry brandy over ice cubes in a mixing glass. Stir to mix. Strain into a chilled cocktail glass.

BUTTAFUOCO ▸

SERVES 1
2 measures white tequila
½ measure Galliano
½ measure cherry brandy
½ measure lemon juice
cracked ice
soda water
cocktail cherry

Pour the white tequila, Galliano, cherry brandy and lemon juice over ice cubes and shake vigorously until well frosted. Half fill a highball glass with cracked ice and strain the cocktail over it. Top up with soda water and dress with a cocktail cherry.

AFRICAN MINT

Amarula is a very rich and exotic liqueur, which is best served and drunk really cold – but not on ice because that will dilute its real character.

SERVES 1
¾ measure crème de menthe, chilled
¾ measure Amarula, chilled

Pour the crème de menthe into the base of a shot glass, saving a few drops. Pour the Amarula slowly over the back of a spoon to create a layer over the minty liquid. Drizzle any remaining drops of mint over the creamy liqueur to finish.

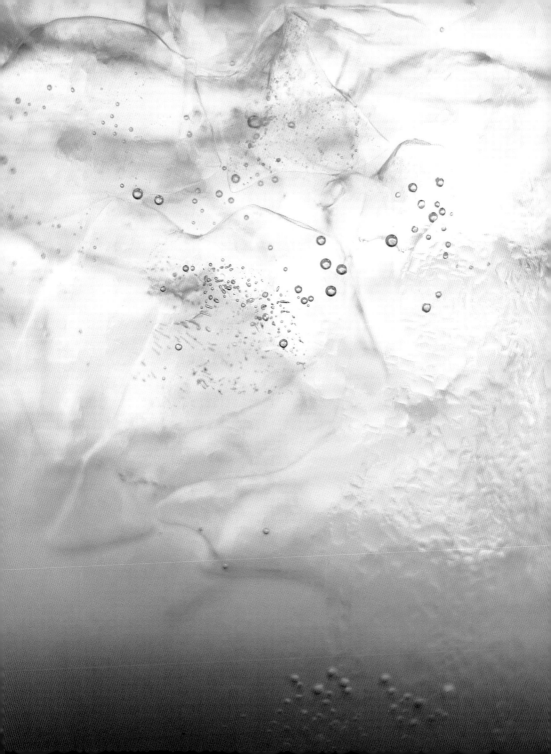

TEQUILA SHOT

SERVES 1
1 measure gold tequila
pinch of salt
lime wedge

Put one measure of gold tequila in a shot glass. Put the salt at the base of your thumb, between thumb and forefinger. Hold the lime wedge in the same hand. Hold the shot of gold tequila in the other hand. Lick the salt, down the tequila and suck the lime.

According to custom the Tequila Shot is the only way to drink neat tequila. It is often described as being smooth and tart, so adding lime juice and salt may sound contradictory, but it works.

GREEN LADY ▲

SERVES 1
2 measures gin
1 measure green Chartreuse
dash of lime juice

Pour the gin, green Chartreuse and dash of lime juice over ice cubes and shake vigorously until well frosted. Strain into a chilled cocktail glass.

While less popular than peach or cherry eau de vie, pear brandy has a delicate fragrance and lovely flavour, but don't confuse it with pear liqueur.

AMERICAN ROLLS-ROYCE ▲

SERVES 1
2 measures brandy
2 measures orange juice
1 measure triple sec

Shake the brandy, orange juice and triple sec over ice cubes until well frosted. Strain into a chilled lowball glass.

PEARTINI

SERVES 1
1 tsp caster sugar
pinch of ground cinnamon
lemon wedge
cracked ice
1 measure vodka
1 measure pear brandy, such as Poire William
   or Pera Segnana

Mix the sugar and cinnamon together on a saucer. Rub the outside rim of a cocktail glass with the lemon wedge, then dip the glass into the sugar and cinnamon mixture. Set aside. Put the cracked ice into a mixing glass or jug and pour in the vodka and pear brandy. Strain into the cocktail glass and serve.

GUMDROP MARTINI ‹

SERVES 1
lemon wedge
caster sugar
2 measures lemon rum
1 measure vodka
½ measure Southern Comfort
½ measure lemon juice
½ tsp dry vermouth
gumdrops or other jelly-like sweets

Rub the rim of a chilled cocktail glass with a wedge of lemon, then dip the glass in a saucer of caster sugar. Vigorously shake the lemon rum, vodka, Southern Comfort, lemon juice and dry vermouth over ice cubes until well frosted. Strain into the prepared glass. Dress with gumdrops.

NUCLEAR FALLOUT

This is similar to a Pousse-Café (page 231), where the liqueurs are layered.

SERVES 1
1 tsp raspberry syrup
¼ measure of maraschino
¼ measure of yellow Chartreuse
¼ measure Cointreau
½ measure well-chilled blue curaçao

Chill all the liqueurs, but especially the blue curaçao – put it in the coldest part of the freezer. Also chill a shot, or pousse-café glass. Carefully pour the raspberry syrup, then the maraschino, yellow Chartreuse and Cointreau in layers over the back of a teaspoon. Finally, pour in the blue curaçao and wait for the fallout.

BLUE LADY

SERVES 1
2½ measures blue curaçao
1 measure white crème de cacao
1 measure single cream

Shake the blue curaçao, white crème de cacao and single cream over ice cubes until well frosted. Strain into a chilled cocktail glass.

ZOMBIE ◄

SERVES 1
crushed ice
2 measures dark rum
2 measures white rum
1 measure golden rum
1 measure triple sec
1 measure lime juice
1 measure orange juice
1 tbsp grenadine
1 tbsp orgeat syrup
1 tsp Pernod

*Put crushed ice in a blender with the dark rum, white rum,
golden rum, triple sec, fruit juice, grenadine, orgeat syrup
and Pernod. Blend until smooth. Pour, without straining,
into a chilled highball glass.*

ZIPPER

This shooter gets its name from an unusual, not to say
'louche' method of serving it, but it tastes just as good
served more conventionally.

SERVES 1
crushed ice
1 measure tequila
½ measure Grand Marnier
½ measure single cream

*Vigorously shake the tequila, Grand Marnier and cream
over the crushed ice for 10–20 seconds, until the outside
of the shaker is misted. Strain into a shot glass.*

BARBED WIRE ►

SERVES 1
3 measures vodka
1 tsp sweet vermouth
½ tsp Pernod
½ measure dry sherry
twist of lemon peel

*Shake the vodka, sweet vermouth, Pernod and dry
sherry over ice cubes until well frosted. Strain into a
chilled wine glass or cocktail glass and dress with a twist
of lemon peel.*

ROYAL MATADOR ◄

SERVES 2
1 pineapple
8–10 ice cubes, crushed
4 measures golden tequila
1½ measures crème de framboise
2 measures lime juice
1 tbsp amaretto
star fruit slice

Cut the top off the pineapple and reserve the lid. Scoop out the flesh, leaving the shell intact. Put the flesh in a blender and purée. Strain the juice from the purée and return it to the blender. Add the crushed ice, golden tequila, crème de framboise, lime juice and amaretto. Blend until slushy, then pour into the pineapple shell, adding more ice if required. Replace the lid and serve with straws and a slice of star fruit.

ORANGE PLANTER'S PUNCH

SERVES 1
1 measure rum
1 measure orange curaçao
2 dashes of Angostura bitters
1 tsp grenadine
juice of 1–2 limes
cracked ice

Vigorously shake the rum, orange curaçao, Angostura bitters, grenadine and lime juice over ice cubes until well frosted. Half fill a chilled highball glass with cracked ice and strain the cocktail over it.

WHITE SPIDER ◄

If you've drunk your fill of cocktails and are thinking about heading home, this is a good one with which to finish the evening off.

SERVES 1
1 measure vodka
1 measure white crème de menthe

Pour the vodka and white crème de menthe over ice cubes in a mixing glass. Stir well and strain into a chilled cocktail glass.

AFTER FIVE

Originally the name of a mixed cocktail topped up with lemonade or soda, the After Five has now been completely transformed into a layered shooter with a real kick.

SERVES 1
½ measure peppermint schnapps, chilled
1 measure Kahlúa, chilled
1 tbsp Baileys Irish Cream, chilled

Pour the peppermint schnapps into a shot glass. Carefully pour the Kahlúa over the back of a teaspoon so that it forms a separate layer. Finally, float the Baileys Irish Cream on top.

SUBMARINO ▸

SERVES 1
250 ml/8 fl oz Mexican beer
2 measures white tequila

Pour the Mexican beer into a chilled beer glass or tankard. Then pour the white tequila into a chilled shot glass and gently submerge the shot glass in the beer.

TEQUINI ▸

As the name suggests, this is a rather nice version of the Martini, which uses tequila instead of gin or vodka.

SERVES 1
cracked ice
3 measures white tequila
½ measure dry vermouth
dash of Angostura bitters
twist of lemon

Pour the white tequila and dry vermouth over cracked ice in a mixing glass. Add the dash of Angostura bitters and stir well. Strain into a chilled martini or cocktail glass and dress with a twist of lemon.

NELL GWYNNE ‹

Nell Gwynne was famously the mistress of 17th-century English king Charles II. When he first met her she was an orange-seller in London's Covent Garden, so it is not surprising that a cocktail named after her is based on the orange-flavoured liqueur triple sec.

SERVES 1
1 measure triple sec
1 measure peach schnapps
1 measure white crème de menthe
twist of lemon peel

Pour the triple sec, peach schnapps and white crème de menthe over ice cubes in a mixing glass and stir well. Strain into a chilled cocktail glass and decorate with a twist of lemon peel.

NEGRONI

SERVES 1
1 measure gin
1 measure sweet vermouth
1 measure Campari
soda water
orange slice

Pour the gin, sweet vermouth and Campari over ice cubes and shake vigorously. Strain into a chilled cocktail glass, top up with soda water if desired and decorate with a slice of orange.

CHOCOLATE MARTINI ‹

SERVES 1
cocoa powder
slice of orange
2 measures vodka
¼ measure crème de cacao
2 dashes orange flower water
twist of orange peel

Moisten the rim of a cocktail glass with an orange slice. Dip in cocoa powder and set aside.

Shake the vodka, crème de cacao and orange flower water over ice cubes until really well frosted. Strain into the cocktail glass and decorate with a twist of orange peel.

THE HAWKSMOOR

LONDON

Although it bears the name of an English baroque architect and evinces the scruffy-chic style of London's trendy Shoreditch district, this East End bar has built its world-class reputation on a classic American cocktail list. Its beautiful cocktail menu is relatively brief, with around 50 choices. However, among them are an entire section of bourbon-based Juleps, alongside a peppering of Algonquins, Brooklyns, Manhattans, Old-fashioneds and Sours.

Many of these drinks date back to the US deep south before Prohibition and while the Hawksmoor is against overly complicated drinks – its Kentucky Mint Julep, for example, uses mint infused in sugar syrup, bourbon and nothing else – it does like to produce its

BEST FOR
classic American cocktails

LIQUORICE WHISKEY SOUR

This version of the traditional Whiskey Sour is a great example of how to evolve a classic effectively. To make the liquorice syrup, put one cup of water and one cup of caster sugar in a pan and bring to the boil. Then add three to four sticks of chopped liquorice root and bring back to the boil. Cool and fine-strain.

SERVES 1

2 measures Buffalo
  Trace bourbon
25 ml/1 fl oz liquorice syrup
dash of Angostura bitters
dash of egg white
grated liquorice root

Shake together the bourbon, liquorice syrup, Angostura bitters and egg white over ice cubes, and double-strain the liquid into a small coupette glass. Garnish with grated liquorice root.

❖

'I think it's legitimate to say that the US invented the cocktail, but cocktails evolve over time and you can choose where you want to dip into that history.'

General manager, Nick Strangeway

own modern twists. General manager and celebrity mixologist Nick Strangeway is a firm believer in updating the classics for modern consumers. The Juleps, Algonquins (a pineapple-flavoured favourite of writer and wit Dorothy Parker) and Sours, for example, are based on darker spirits such as rum, bourbon and rye whiskey. However, the award-winning staff have had a little lightheaded fun with a couple of gin fizzes too.

The place's playful sense of humour is also conveyed in its kitschy tweeked Tikis with names like Leilani's Grass Hut, plus some world-beating punches, of which Strangeway is the grand master, all served up in an eclectic collection of vintage glassware that fits perfectly with the brick interior and long teak bar, salvaged from a 1930s dancehall. Nicholas Hawksmoor, who designed Christ Church Spitalfields just down the road, probably wouldn't know what to make of it.

THE HAWKSMOOR
157 Commercial Street
London E1 6BJ
+44 20 7247 7392
www.thehawksmoor.com

Open Monday to Saturday
Monday, Tuesday and Wednesday
12.00 p.m. to 12.00 a.m.
Thursday and Friday
12.00 p.m. to 1.00 a.m.
Saturday
6.00 p.m. to 1.00 a.m.

PARTY INVITATION

If you're the host, you'll find recipes here that will impress when made in volume, as well as recipes that will stun when made on an individual basis. All are guaranteed to make your party go with that elusive swing. So if you're a guest, simply raise your cocktail glass and enjoy.

CAIPIRINHA ‹

This classic Brazilian cocktail is based on the sugar cane spirit cachaça. If you find it too sharp, add a little more sugar.

SERVES 1
6 lime wedges
2 tsp granulated sugar
3 measures cachaça
cracked ice
lime wedge

Put the lime wedges and sugar in a chilled lowball glass, and muddle them to release the lime juice. Pour on the cachaça, fill up the glass with cracked ice and stir well. Serve with a wedge of lime.

The name 'Caipirinha' translates loosely as 'country bumpkin' or 'hillbilly'. However, the Caipirinha cocktail – which is often described as the national drink of Brazil – is now popular around the world, and is actually a sophisticated drink that delivers quite a kick.

The key to making a good Caipirinha is the way you muddle the limes and the sugar, to release the oils from the fruit peel.

Premium quality cachaça is now available in most off-licences but, if you can't find it, use vodka and make a Caipiroska instead. If you've got rum, make a Caipirissima. If you find either of these too sharp, add a little more sugar. Another variant is the Caipifruta, which consists of cachaça, just about any crushed fresh fruit or fruits, condensed milk and crushed ice.

MARGARITA JELLY SHOT

SERVES 10
3 lime wedges
2 tbsp fine salt
1 packet lime jelly
300 ml / 10 fl oz hot water
4–5 tbsp Cointreau
200–250 ml / 7–9 fl oz tequila

Rub the outside rims of ten shot glasses with the lime wedges, then dip in the salt to frost them. Set aside. Break up the jelly and place it in a heatproof measuring jug. Pour in the hot water and stir until the jelly has dissolved. Leave until cool, then stir in the Cointreau and tequila to make the mixture up to 600 ml (1 pint). Divide the jelly liquid among the prepared glasses, taking care not to disturb the salt frosting, and chill in the refrigerator until set.

It is not essential to frost the glasses with salt for the Margarita Jelly Shot, but it does look attractive and pays homage to the original classic Margarita cocktail recipe of 1942.

TEQUILA COCKTAIL ▲

SERVES 1
dash of Angostura bitters
3 measures golden tequila
1 measure lime juice
½ measure grenadine

Pour the dash of Angostura bitters, golden tequila, lime juice and grenadine over ice cubes and shake vigorously until well frosted, then strain into a chilled cocktail glass.

IRISH EYES ›

SERVES 1

4–6 ice cubes, cracked

2 measures Irish whiskey

½ measure green Chartreuse

Put the cracked ice into a mixing glass. Pour the Irish whiskey and green Chartreuse over the ice. Stir well and strain into a chilled cocktail or lowball glass.

MILLIONAIRE COCKTAIL ›

SERVES 1

⅔ measure bourbon

⅓ measure Cointreau

2 dashes of grenadine

1 egg white

Shake the bourbon, Cointreau, grenadine and egg white over ice cubes and strain into a cocktail glass.

EL DIABLO ▶

One or two Diablos and you'll certainly feel a bit of a devil, but one or two too many and you'll feel like the very devil.

SERVES 1
cracked ice
2–3 strips of lime peel
1 measure lime juice
3 measures white tequila
1 measure crème de cassis
twist of lime peel

Fill a chilled lowball glass with the cracked ice, add the lime peel, lime juice, tequila and crème de cassis. Stir well to mix. Serve with a twist of lime peel.

CHRISTMAS PUNCH ▲

SERVES 8
1 litre/1¾ pints red wine
4 tbsp sugar
1 cinnamon stick
400 ml/14 fl oz boiling water
100 ml/3½ fl oz brandy
100 ml/3½ fl oz sherry
100 ml/3½ fl oz orange liqueur
2 seedless oranges, cut into wedges
2 dessert apples, cored and cut into wedges

Put the wine, sugar and cinnamon into a large pan. Warm over a low heat, stirring, until the mixture just starts to simmer, but don't allow it to boil. Remove from the heat and strain. Discard the cinnamon stick. Return the wine to the pan and add the remaining ingredients. Warm gently over a very low heat. Serve hot in heatproof glasses.

In the bleak midwinter a glass of this piping hot Christmas Punch will warm the cockles of anyone's heart. Remember, do not allow the mixture to boil as you will burn off all the alcohol. Simmer gently.

SCREWDRIVER

This cocktail has universal appeal, and is great to serve to guests at a party if you're not sure of individual tastes. Freshly squeezed orange juice is a must.

SERVES 1
cracked ice
2 measures vodka
orange juice
orange slice

Fill a chilled highball glass with the cracked ice. Pour the vodka over the ice and top up with orange juice. Stir well to mix and dress with a slice of orange.

A number of cocktails are known simply by their initials. In this classic recipe BVD stands for brandy, vermouth and Dubonnet. Strangely, although it retains the name, a modern BVD contains white rum, gin and dry vermouth.

BVD

SERVES 1
cracked ice
1 measure brandy
1 measure dry vermouth
1 measure Dubonnet

Pour the brandy, dry vermouth and Dubonnet over cracked ice in a mixing glass. Stir to mix and strain into a chilled cocktail glass.

DIAMOND HEAD

SERVES 2

4 measures gin

2 measures lemon juice

1 measure apricot brandy

1 tsp sugar

1 egg white

spirals of lemon peel

Pour the gin, lemon juice, apricot brandy, sugar and egg white over ice cubes and shake vigorously until well frosted. Strain into two chilled cocktail glasses and serve with spirals of lemon peel.

LEAP YEAR

SERVES 1

2 measures gin

½ measure Grand Marnier

½ measure sweet vermouth

½ tsp lemon juice

Pour the gin, Grand Marnier, sweet vermouth and lemon juice over ice cubes and shake vigorously until well frosted. Strain into a chilled cocktail glass.

CHAMPAGNE SIDECAR ◄

SERVES 1
4–6 ice cubes, cracked
2 measures brandy
1 measure triple sec
1 measure lemon juice
champagne, chilled
twist of orange peel

Vigorously shake the brandy, triple sec and lemon juice over the cracked ice until a frost forms. Strain into a chilled flute and top it up with chilled champagne. Dress with a twist of orange peel.

SANGRÍA

A perfect long cold drink for a summer party.

SERVES 6
juice of 1 orange
juice of 1 lemon
2 tbsp caster sugar
1 orange, thinly sliced
1 lemon, thinly sliced
1 bottle red wine, chilled
lemonade

Stir the orange juice, lemon juice and sugar together in a large bowl or jug. When the sugar has dissolved, add a few ice cubes, the sliced orange and lemon, and the wine. Marinate for one hour, then add lemonade and a few more ice cubes. Serve in wine glasses or highball glasses.

Cointreau is the best-known brand of orange-flavoured liqueur, but the Champagne Sidecar calls for triple sec, which is drier and stronger than curaçao and always colourless.

Make the stunning ice cubes required by the Louisa well in advance and only take out of the freezer at the very last second – they melt almost immediately.

LOUISA ▲

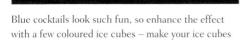

Blue cocktails look such fun, so enhance the effect with a few coloured ice cubes – make your ice cubes with a couple of drops of blue food colouring.

SERVES 1
6–8 ice cubes, cracked
¾ measure blue curaçao
½ measure vodka
¼ measure barley water
dash of lemon juice
soda water
blue ice cubes (see above)

Fill a highball glass with the cracked ice, add the blue curaçao, vodka, barley water and lemon juice, and mix well. Top up with soda water and finish with blue ice cubes.

MINTED DIAMONDS ▸

SERVES 1
1 tsp green crème de menthe
1 tbsp iced water
1 measure white crème de menthe
2 measures apple or pear schnapps

Mix the green crème de menthe with the iced water, spoon the mixture into one or two compartments of an ice cube tray and freeze for about two hours. Stir the white crème de menthe and apple or pear schnapps over ice cubes until well frosted. Strain the liquid into a chilled cocktail glass and float the mint ice cubes on top at the last moment. Don't start drinking until the mint cubes begin to melt.

BRANDY COCKTAIL

SERVES 1
dash of Angostura bitters
2 measures brandy
½ tsp sugar syrup
lemon peel

Pour the dash of Angostura bitters, brandy and sugar syrup over ice cubes and shake vigorously until well frosted. Strain into a chilled cocktail glass and decorate with a twist of lemon peel.

MELANIE HAMILTON ◄

SERVES 1
2 measures triple sec
1 measure Midori
2 measures orange juice
cantaloupe melon wedge

Pour the triple sec, Midori and orange juice over ice cubes and shake vigorously until well frosted. Strain the mixture into a chilled cocktail glass and dress with a wedge of cantaloupe melon.

NAVAJO TRAIL ▲

SERVES 1
2 measures white tequila
1 measure triple sec
1 measure lime juice
1 measure cranberry juice

Pour the white tequila, triple sec, lime juice and cranberry juice over ice cubes and shake vigorously until well frosted. Strain into a chilled cocktail glass.

WHISKEY SLING ▾

SERVES 1
1 tsp sugar
1 measure lemon juice
1 tsp water
2 measures American blended whiskey
cracked ice
orange slice

In a mixing glass, stir the sugar, lemon juice and water together until the sugar has dissolved. Pour in the American blended whiskey and stir to mix. Half fill a chilled lowball glass with the cracked ice and strain the cocktail over it. Dress with an orange slice.

QUEEN OF MEMPHIS ▸

SERVES 1
2 measures bourbon
1 measure Midori
1 measure peach juice
dash of maraschino
melon wedge

Pour the bourbon, Midori, peach juice and dash of maraschino over ice cubes and shake vigorously until well frosted. Strain into a chilled cocktail glass and dress with a wedge of melon.

PEPPERMINT PATTY

Sometimes the simple things in life are the best – one such pleasure is this delicious combination of chocolate and peppermint.

SERVES 1
1 measure white crème de cacao
1 measure white crème de menthe

Vigorously shake the crème de cacao and crème de menthe over ice cubes for 10–20 seconds, until the outside of the shaker is misted. Strain into a shot glass or cocktail glass.

PINK HEATHER ▸

SERVES 1

1 measure Scotch whisky
1 measure strawberry liqueur
sparkling wine, chilled
1 strawberry

Pour the Scotch whisky and strawberry liqueur into a chilled champagne flute. Top up with the chilled sparkling wine and dress with the strawberry.

SHILLELAGH ◂

A shillelagh (pronounced shee-lay-lee) is a wooden cudgel, traditionally made from blackthorn. Undoubtedly, this is a cocktail that hits the spot.

SERVES 1

2 measures Irish whiskey
1 measure dry sherry
1 tsp golden rum
1 tsp lemon juice
pinch of caster sugar
cocktail cherry

Pour the Irish whiskey, dry sherry, golden rum, lemon juice and pinch of caster sugar over ice cubes and shake vigorously until well frosted. Strain into a chilled cocktail glass and dress with a cocktail cherry.

BRAIN HAEMORRHAGE

This is a rare instance of a cocktail that is deliberately intended to look unpleasant, rather than tempting. It was probably invented to drink at Halloween.

SERVES 1

1 measure peach schnapps, chilled
1 tsp Baileys Irish Cream, chilled
½ tsp grenadine, chilled

Pour the peach schnapps into a shot glass, then carefully float the Baileys on top. Finally, top with the grenadine.

BULLDOG BREED ▸

SERVES 1
cracked ice
1 measure gin
2 measures orange juice
ginger ale, chilled

Half fill a chilled highball glass or lowball glass with cracked ice. Pour the gin and orange juice over and top up with chilled ginger ale. Stir.

AROUND THE WORLD ▴

SERVES 1
1 measure Mandarine Napoleon
1 measure Polish vodka
½ measure Campari
½ measure crème de banane
½ measure coconut liqueur
cracked ice
lemonade
kumquats, halved

Shake the Mandarine Napoleon, Polish vodka, Campari, crème de banane and coconut liqueur over ice cubes until frosted. Fill a highball or lowball glass with the cracked ice, strain in the liquid and top up with lemonade. Decorate with kumquat halves.

As you can see from the name, flavours from all 'around the world' go into this glorious cocktail, so save it for a cosmopolitan occasion.

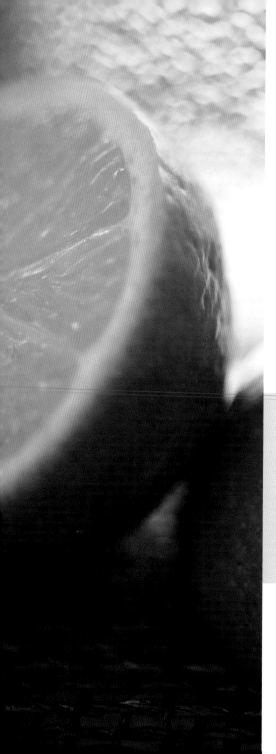

MARGARITA

A number of people claim to have invented the Margarita but what is for certain is that it is now one of the world's most popular cocktails.

SERVES 1
2 lime wedges
salt
3 measures white tequila
1 measure Cointreau or triple sec
2 measures lime juice

Rub the rim of a chilled cocktail glass with one of the wedges of lime and dip the glass into the salt to frost it. Vigorously shake the tequila, Cointreau and lime juice over ice cubes until well frosted. Strain into the prepared glass, squeeze the remaining lime wedge over the top and then drop it in.

The Margarita is a civilised version of the original way to drink tequila – with a lick of salt, a suck of lime juice and a shot of tequila.

SELF-DESTRUCT ▾

SERVES 1
3 measures vodka
½ tsp lime juice
½ tsp triple sec

Shake the vodka, lime juice and triple sec over ice cubes until well frosted. Strain into a chilled cocktail glass

PINK PUSSYCAT ▲

Although it's not the only ingredient you can use, a dash of grenadine will usually give your cocktail a pinky tinge.

SERVES 1
cracked ice
dash of grenadine
2 measures gin
pineapple juice
pineapple slice

Half fill a chilled highball glass with cracked ice. Dash the grenadine over the ice and pour in the gin. Top up with the pineapple juice and dress with a slice of pineapple.

KISS KISS

SERVES 1
cracked ice
1 measure cherry brandy
1 measure gin
1 measure sweet vermouth

Half fill a mixing glass with cracked ice and pour the cherry brandy, gin and sweet vermouth over them. Stir well, then strain into a chilled cocktail glass.

ARTILLERY PUNCH ▸

SERVES 30
1 litre/1¾ pints bourbon
1 litre/1¾ pints red wine
1 litre/1¾ pints strong, black tea
475 ml/16 fl oz dark rum
250 ml/8 fl oz gin
250 ml/8 fl oz apricot brandy
4 measures lemon juice
4 measures lime juice
4 tbsp sugar syrup
large block of ice
orange slices, thinly cut

Pour all the liquids and sugar syrup into a large bowl. Refrigerate for two hours. Place a large block of ice in a punch bowl. Pour the punch over the ice and decorate with slices of orange. Serve in highball glasses.

TAILGATE ◂

SERVES 1
6 ice cubes, cracked
dash of orange bitters
2 measures vodka
1 measure green Chartreuse
1 measure sweet vermouth

Put the cracked ice into a mixing glass. Dash the orange bitters over the ice and pour in the vodka, green Chartreuse and sweet vermouth. Stir well to mix, then strain into a chilled cocktail glass.

PINEAPPLE PLANTER'S PUNCH ‹

SERVES 1
1 measure white rum
1 measure pineapple juice
juice of half a lime
½ measure curaçao
dash of maraschino
cracked ice
kiwi fruit wedge
pineapple wedges

*Mix the white rum, pineapple juice, lime juice, curaçao
and dash of maraschino together. Serve in a highball
glass with cracked ice and fruit wedges.*

The word Sangaree is derived
from the Spanish word
for blood and Sangarees
were once made with wine.
Nowadays, they are more
likely to have a spirit base
– but whatever is used,
the cocktail is invariably
flavoured with fresh nutmeg.

GIN SANGAREE ▲

SERVES 1
6–8 ice cubes, cracked
2 measures gin
½ tsp sugar syrup
sparkling water
1 tbsp port
nutmeg, freshly grated

*Put the cracked ice into a chilled highball glass or lowball
glass. Pour the gin and sugar syrup over the ice and top
up with sparkling water. Stir gently to mix, then float the
port on top. Sprinkle with freshly grated nutmeg.*

TRASHY WOMEN ▸

SERVES 1
2 measures bourbon
1 measure Pernod
1 measure apple juice
dash of Angostura bitters
apple slice

Pour the bourbon, Pernod, apple juice and a dash of Angostura bitters over ice cubes and shake vigorously until well frosted. Strain into a chilled cocktail glass and dress with a slice of apple.

CREOLE LADY

SERVES 1
cracked ice
2 measures bourbon
1½ measures madeira
1 tsp grenadine
cocktail cherries

Pour the bourbon, madeira and grenadine over cracked ice in a mixing glass. Stir well to mix, then strain into a chilled cocktail glass. Dress with cocktail cherries.

PINK WHISKERS ▸

SERVES 1
2 measures apricot brandy
1 measure dry vermouth
2 measures orange juice
dash of grenadine

Shake the apricot brandy, dry vermouth, orange juice and a dash of grenadine vigorously over ice cubes until well frosted. Strain the mixture into a chilled cocktail glass.

SOUTHERN PEACH ◂

SERVES 1
cracked ice
1 measure Southern Comfort
1 measure peach brandy
1 measure single cream
dash of Angostura bitters
peach slice

Pour the Southern Comfort, peach brandy, single cream and a dash of Angostura bitters over cracked ice and shake vigorously until well frosted. Strain the mixture into a chilled cocktail glass or lowball glass and dress with a slice of peach.

TROPICAL FRUIT PUNCH ▾

SERVES 6
1 small ripe mango
4 tbsp lime juice
1 tsp fresh ginger, finely grated
1 tbsp light brown sugar
300 ml/10 fl oz orange juice
300 ml/10 fl oz pineapple juice
80 ml/3 fl oz rum
crushed ice
orange slices
lime slices
pineapple slices
pineapple leaves
star fruit slices

Blend the mango with the lime juice, ginger and sugar until smooth. Add the fruit juices and rum, and process again for a few seconds. Pour over the ice and dress with the fruit.

The Tropical Fruit Punch is simplicity itself and can be varied with different fruit juices. Top with lavish amounts of fruit for a really festive effect and if you want a great long drink, add ginger ale.

Thanksgiving is a traditional North American celebration to mark and give thanks for the end of the harvest, but even if you don't celebrate it, the Thanksgiving Special will go down well at any autumn or winter party.

THANKSGIVING SPECIAL

SERVES 1
2 measures gin
1½ measures apricot brandy
1 measure dry vermouth
½ measure lemon juice

Pour the gin, apricot brandy, dry vermouth and lemon juice over ice cubes and shake vigorously until well frosted. Strain into a chilled cocktail glass.

COOL YULE MARTINI ▸

A seasonal variation on the classic. Ideal, of course, for serving to guests at a Christmas party.

SERVES 1
3 measures vodka
½ measure dry vermouth
1 tsp peppermint schnapps
sprig of fresh mint

Shake the vodka, dry vermouth and peppermint schnapps over ice cubes until well frosted. Strain into a chilled martini or cocktail glass and dress with a sprig of fresh mint.

OK CORRAL ‹

SERVES 1

2 measures rye whiskey

1 measure grapefruit juice

1 tsp orgeat syrup

Pour the rye whiskey, grapefruit juice and orgeat syrup over ice cubes and shake vigorously until well frosted. Strain into a chilled cocktail glass.

As long as they are different colours and well chilled, you can use any combination of liqueurs in the Traffic Light.

TRAFFIC LIGHT ›

SERVES 1

crushed ice

½–1 measure mint brandy, chilled

½–1 measure orange brandy, chilled

½–1 measure cherry brandy, chilled

Fill a wine glass or a cocktail glass with crushed ice. Then carefully, in order, pour in the chilled mint, orange and, finally, the cherry brandy.

TRETTER'S BAR

PRAGUE

Perverse as it might seem to head for a cocktail bar in a city renowned for its beer, Tretter's in Prague gives Bohemian pubs a run for their money with its much-praised selection of house drinks. Its list of cocktails includes 60 time-honoured classics. The remainder are its own creations, devised by its award-winning owner Michael Tretter and his highly trained bar staff.

In appearance, this is an old-school cocktail bar, with a deep red interior, leather loungers and a long bar. In Prague's Old Town Jewish district, it harks back to the Art Deco period. Yet, despite its own stylish look and a sprinkling of fashionista clientele, it is still remarkably relaxed and laid back. It is true it doesn't open its

BEST FOR
house cocktails

JEAN GABIN

During cold winter evenings, Tretter's is fond of serving mulled wine with a twist, adding badyan or star anise. This rum and brandy-based drink is also a favourite for when the mercury drops.

SERVES 1

44 ml/1½ fl oz dark rum
22 ml/¾ fl oz Calvados
1 tbsp maple or
    almond syrup
150 ml/5 fl oz hot milk
pinch of nutmeg

Heat the rum, Calvados and syrup. Fold in the hot milk and pour into a heat-resistant glass. Sprinkle with the nutmeg.

◆

'Bartending is a Tretter family tradition, passed from father to son for 90 years, so it's natural to have a bit of a nostalgic feeling in the bar, evoking 1930s New York or Paris.'

Owner, Michael Tretter

doors to large stag parties, but the policy is otherwise welcoming, egalitarian and without any dress code.

Small wonder then that the pioneering Tretter's, which started up just as the Czech capital began to emerge as a leading tourist destination, still consistently wins the best cocktail bar award, as voted for annually by readers of the *Prague Post*.

Champagne cocktails always get the thumbs-up here, including Rose's Time made from peach liquor, raspberries, Rose's lime juice, Ciroc vodka and sparkling wine. Among its popular house cocktails you'll find Thai Parade, a concoction of lychee liqueur, Ciroc vodka, red berry syrup and lemon juice. Mojitos and Cuba Libres are other solid choices, although Tretter's stands out by often adding ginger, basil or rosemary.

Finally, for those who reckon a visit to Prague just wouldn't be complete without it, Tretter's also serves beer…

TRETTER'S BAR

V kolkovni 3
110 00 Prague 1
+420 224 811 165
www.tretters.cz

Open daily
7.00 p.m.–3.00 a.m.

END OF THE EVENING

As the lights dim and the evening finally draws to a close, do you prefer to go out in a blaze of glory with one last blast? Or do you prefer to wind down with a relaxing warm drink that will send you off to sleep? Whichever style you favour, you'll find the solution here.

AMARETTO COFFEE ◂

This is a lovely variation on Irish Coffee. Amaretto is a deliciously sweet, almond-flavoured liqueur made from apricot kernels. It is delicious drunk on its own, but also forms the basis of a number of cocktails.

SERVES 1
1 cup hot black coffee
2 tbsp amaretto
1–2 tbsp double cream

Stir the amaretto into the hot coffee. Then carefully pour the cream on top over the back of a spoon to form a layer

For once there is a fair degree of agreement about who invented a cocktail and the Irish Coffee is attributed, more or less without dispute, to a chef called Joe Sheridan, who worked at what is now Shannon International Airport in the west of Ireland in the 1940s. One cold and dank evening he apparently decided to cheer up some Americans who'd just arrived by adding whiskey to their coffee. The Americans asked if they were being served Brazilian Coffee, to which Sheridan replied that it was Irish Coffee.

An Amaretto Coffee is usually served in an Irish Coffee glass, which is a heatproof, short-stemmed glass vessel with a handle, but any heatproof glass will do.

WHITE DIAMOND FRAPPÉ

This is a crazy combination of liqueurs, but it works well once you've added the lemon. Extra crushed ice at the last minute brings out all the separate flavours.

SERVES 1
crushed ice
¼ measure peppermint schnapps
¼ measure white crème de cacao
¼ measure anise liqueur
¼ measure lemon juice

Shake the peppermint schnapps, white crème de cacao, anise liqueur and lemon juice over some of the crushed ice until frosted. Strain into a chilled cocktail glass and add a small extra spoonful of crushed ice.

HOT BRANDY CHOCOLATE ▸

Brandy and chocolate certainly do have a natural affinity, as this delicious drink demonstrates.

SERVES 4
1 litre/1¾ pints milk
115 g/4 oz dark chocolate, broken into pieces
2 tbsp sugar
5 tbsp brandy
6 tbsp whipped cream
grated nutmeg or cocoa powder

Pour the milk into a pan and bring to the boil, then remove from the heat. Add the chocolate and sugar, and stir over a low heat until the chocolate has melted. Pour into four heatproof glasses and then pour the brandy over a spoon on to the top of each one. Finish with a swirl of cream and a sprinkling of nutmeg or cocoa powder.

WHAT THE DICKENS? ◂

SERVES 1
2 measures gin
1½ tsp icing sugar
hot water
twist of lemon peel

Pour the gin into a heatproof glass and stir in the icing sugar. Top up with hot water and serve with a twist of lemon peel.

RATTLESNAKE ‹

SERVES 1

1 measure Baileys Irish Cream, chilled
1 measure dark crème de cacao, chilled
1 measure Kahlúa, chilled

*Pour the chilled Baileys Irish Cream into a shot glass
With a steady hand, gently pour in the chilled dark
crème de cacao to make a second layer and then
gently pour in the chilled Kahlúa to make a third layer.
Do not stir.*

HAZY LADY

The bright pink grenadine soon trickles through these
rich nutty-flavoured liqueurs to give a pretty base layer.

SERVES 1

½ measure crème de noyau
½ measure coffee liqueur
½ measure brandy
½ measure orange juice
dash of egg white
dash of grenadine
grated nutmeg

*Shake together the crème de noyau, coffee liqueur,
brandy, orange juice and egg white over ice cubes until
frosted. Strain into an iced cocktail glass, and dress with
a dash of grenadine and a sprinkling of grated nutmeg*

Instead of hot chocolate,
the small but flamboyant
emperor of France, Napoleon
Bonaparte, apparently
favoured this chocolate-laced
brandy with a hint of banana
for a nightcap. Daring
and extravagant.

NAPOLEON'S NIGHTCAP

SERVES 1

1¼ measures cognac
1 measure dark crème de cacao
¼ measure crème de banane
1 tbsp single cream

*Stir the cognac, dark crème de cacao and crème
de banane together in a mixing glass with ice cubes.
Strain into a chilled cocktail glass and spoon on a layer
of cream.*

IRISH STINGER ▶

SERVES 1
1 measure Baileys Irish Cream
1 measure white crème de menthe

Pour the Baileys Irish Cream and white crème de menthe over ice cubes, shake vigorously until well frosted, and strain into a chilled shot or lowball glass.

HEAVENLY ▲

SERVES 1
cracked ice
1½ measures brandy
½ measure cherry brandy
½ measure plum brandy
olives

Put the cracked ice into a mixing glass and pour the brandy, cherry brandy and plum brandy over it. Stir well to mix and strain into a chilled cocktail glass or brandy snifter. Serve with a couple of olives on a cocktail stick.

SPOTTED BIKINI

A cheeky name for an amusing cocktail, but it also tastes great, although you may like to add a little sugar to taste.

SERVES 1
2 measures vodka
1 measure white rum
1 measure cold milk
juice of ½ lemon
1 ripe passion fruit
lemon slice

Shake the vodka, white rum, milk and lemon juice over ice cubes until well frosted. Strain into a chilled medium cocktail glass and add the pulp of the passion fruit, unstrained, at the last minute so you can see the black seeds – or spots. Dress with a slice of lemon.

PORT WINE COBBLER ▾

SERVES 1
1 tsp caster sugar
2 measures sparkling water
cracked ice
3 measures ruby port
orange slice
cocktail cherry

*Put the sugar into a chilled wine glass and add the
sparkling water. Stir until the sugar has dissolved. Fill the
glass with cracked ice and pour in the ruby port. Dress
with a slice of orange and a cocktail cherry.*

SPICED HOT CHOCOLATE

This is a treat after an evening spent singing carols on
Christmas Eve.

SERVES 4
850 ml/1½ pints milk
200 g/7 oz good dark chocolate (at least 70% cocoa
    solids), broken into pieces
2 tsp sugar
1 tsp mixed spice
4 sticks cinnamon
2 tbsp whipped cream

*Put the milk, chocolate, sugar and mixed spice into a
saucepan over a medium heat. Whisk until the mixture
is simmering, but not boiling. Remove from the heat and
pour into heatproof glasses or mugs, add cinnamon
sticks and top with a little whipped cream.*

PINK ALMOND ▸

SERVES 1

2 measures blended American whiskey
1 measure amaretto
½ measure crème de noyau
½ measure cherry brandy
1 measure lemon juice
lemon slice

Pour the blended American whiskey, amaretto, crème de noyau, cherry brandy and lemon juice over ice cubes and shake vigorously until well frosted. Strain into a chilled goblet and dress with a slice of lemon.

SCOTCH SANGAREE ▸

SERVES 1

1 tsp clear honey
sparkling water
cracked ice
2 measures Scotch whisky
spiral of lemon peel
freshly grated nutmeg

Put the honey in a chilled lowball glass with a little sparkling water and stir until dissolved. Add cracked ice and the Scotch whisky, and top up with more sparkling water. Stir gently to mix, then decorate with a spiral of lemon peel and freshly grated nutmeg.

TIGER'S MILK ‹

SERVES 1
2 measures golden rum
1½ measures brandy
1 tsp sugar syrup
150 ml/5 fl oz milk
crushed ice
ground cinnamon
cinnamon stick

Blend the golden rum, brandy, sugar syrup and milk with crushed ice until combined. Pour into a chilled wine glass or cocktail glass and sprinkle with ground cinnamon. Serve with a cinnamon stick.

ALEXANDER

A creamy, chocolate-flavoured, gin-based cocktail, decorated with grated nutmeg.

SERVES 1
1 measure gin
1 measure crème de cacao
1 measure single cream
freshly grated nutmeg

Pour the gin, crème de cacao and single cream over ice cubes and shake vigorously until well frosted. Strain into a chilled cocktail glass and dress with freshly grated nutmeg.

OLD FASHIONED

This delicious recipe is a perfect illustration of the saying, 'Sometimes the old ones are the best.'

SERVES 1
1 sugar cube
dash of Angostura bitters
1 tsp water
2 measures bourbon or rye whiskey
cracked ice
lemon peel

Place the sugar cube in a small, chilled old-fashioned or lowball glass, then add the dash of Angostura bitters and water. Mash with a spoon until the sugar has dissolved, then pour in the whiskey and stir. Add cracked ice and decorate with a twist of lemon peel.

BOURBON COBBLER ▸

SERVES 1

1 tsp caster sugar

dash of lemon juice

6 ice cubes, cracked

2 measures bourbon

2 measures Southern Comfort

soda water

peach slice

Put the caster sugar and lemon juice into a chilled highball glass. Add the cracked ice, bourbon and Southern Comfort. Top up with soda water and stir to mix. Dress with a slice of peach.

MOONRISE ▲

SERVES 1

300 ml/10 fl oz medium dry cider

1 tbsp brown sugar

pinch of ground cinnamon

pinch of freshly grated nutmeg

1 measure apple brandy

2 tsp single cream

Put the cider into a saucepan with the brown sugar, a pinch of ground cinnamon and a pinch of freshly grated nutmeg. Heat gently, stirring until the sugar has dissolved. Pour into a warmed heatproof glass and stir in the apple brandy. Float the single cream on top by pouring gently over the back of a teaspoon.

SALOME

Dark, mysterious and very risqué – just like the Dance of the Seven Veils.

SERVES 1

⅓ measure gin

⅓ measure Dubonnet

⅓ measure dry vermouth

cherry or pecan nut

Stir the gin, Dubonnet and dry vermouth together over ice cubes and pour into a chilled cocktail glass, finishing with a cherry.

TAMAGOZAKE ◄

This is a brave drink for a special occasion, but be careful not to burn away all the sake. You might want to blow it out before all the flavour and spirit has been burnt up.

SERVES 1
1 egg
1 tsp sugar
6 measures sake

Beat the egg and sugar together lightly. Boil the sake, ignite it and then remove from the heat. Stir in the egg and sugar mixture and serve in a mug with a handle.

SILVER STREAK

This nightcap can be made with either gin or vodka, but whichever spirit you choose, make sure it is really cold and don't stir – just let the kümmel sink through it.

SERVES 1
4–6 ice cubes, cracked
1 measure gin or vodka, iced
1 measure kümmel, iced

Put the cracked ice in a small old-fashioned or lowball glass and add the gin or vodka. Slowly pour on the kümmel and then drink before the two liquids become too mingled.

HUNGARIAN COFFEE ▲

SERVES 1
2 measures brandy
sugar
strong black coffee, freshly made
1 tbsp chocolate, grated
whipped cream
cinnamon stick

Put the brandy into a warmed heatproof glass and add sugar to taste. Pour in the coffee and grated chocolate, and stir. When the sugar has completely dissolved and the chocolate has melted, top with whipped cream and serve with a stick of cinnamon. Don't stir, drink the coffee through the cream.

MOON LANDING

SERVES 1
1 measure vodka
1 measure Tia Maria
1 measure amaretto
1 measure Baileys Irish Cream

Shake the vodka, Tia Maria, amaretto and Baileys Irish Cream over ice cubes until well frosted. Strain into a chilled shot glass.

KGB

Short for Komityet Gosudarstvyennoi Byezopasnosti, the Soviet Union's notorious intelligence service. Maybe the cocktail was one of the agents' favourite tipples when they fancied a change from vodka.

SERVES 1
1½ measures gin
½ measure kümmel
dash of apricot brandy

Vigorously shake the gin and kümmel over ice cubes with a dash of apricot brandy until well frosted. Strain into a chilled cocktail glass.

PINK SQUIRREL

SERVES 1
cracked ice
2 measures dark crème de cacao
1 measure crème de noyau
1 measure single cream

Pour the crème de cacao, crème de noyau and single cream over the cracked ice and shake vigorously until well frosted. Strain into a chilled cocktail glass.

Crème de noyau has a wonderful, slightly bitter, nutty flavour, but is made from peach and apricot kernels. It is usually served as a liqueur, but does combine well with other ingredients in cocktails like the Pink Squirrel.

WHISKEY RICKEY ▲

SERVES 1
2 measures American blended whiskey
2 measures fresh lime juice
soda water
lime slice

Half fill a highball glass with ice cubes and pour in the whiskey and lime juice. Top up with soda water and dress with a slice of lime.

IRISH COW

SERVES 1
250 ml/8 fl oz milk
2 measures Irish whiskey
1 tsp caster sugar

Heat the milk in a small saucepan to just below boiling point. Remove from the heat and pour into a warmed heatproof glass or mug. Add the Irish whiskey and caster sugar, and stir until the sugar has dissolved.

SLOE GIN RICKEY ▸

The original Rickey is made with gin. Here the sloe gin makes it a slightly sweeter, but still sharp and refreshing, drink.

SERVES 1
2 measures sloe gin
2 measures fresh lime juice
soda water
lime slice

Half fill a highball glass with ice cubes and pour in the sloe gin and lime juice. Top up with soda water and dress with a slice of lime.

WHISKY MAC

This popular classic is enjoyed worldwide as a warming winter drink, so don't be tempted to chill the glass or the drinks.

SERVES 1
1½ measures Scotch whisky
1 measure ginger wine

Carefully pour the Scotch whisky and ginger wine into an old-fashioned glass or lowball glass. Allow them to mix, but don't stir.

ROADRUNNER ◀

Whether it is named after the real bird or after Wile E. Coyote's nemesis, this is a cocktail for slowing down after a fast-moving day, not for speeding things up.

SERVES 1
1 measure vodka
½ measure Malibu
½ measure amaretto

Pour the vodka, Malibu and amaretto over ice cubes and shake vigorously until well frosted. Strain into a chilled cocktail glass.

MEXICAN COFFEE

SERVES 1
2 measures Kahlúa
sugar
strong black coffee, freshly made
whipped cream
chocolate, grated

Put the Kahlúa into a warmed heatproof glass and add sugar to taste. Pour in the coffee and stir. When the sugar has completely dissolved, top with the whipped cream and the grated chocolate. Don't stir, just drink the coffee through the cream.

POLISH SIDECAR ◀

SERVES 1
2 measures gin
1 measure blackberry brandy
1 measure lemon juice
fresh blackberry

Vigorously shake the gin, blackberry brandy and lemon juice over ice cubes until well frosted. Strain into a chilled cocktail glass and decorate with a fresh blackberry.

CSA-BAR

BERLIN

Karl Marx would spin in his grave to see this chic establishment along the socialist-era boulevard bearing his name. In fact, anyone who knew this once rundown East Berlin district of Friedrichshain in the 1990s would be astounded to see its transformation in the 21st century.

Located in the former office of CSA Czech Airlines (from which it takes its name), this sleek minimalist bar has retained the best bits of the original 1950s decor but hasn't been afraid to consign the rest to the dustbin of Cold War history.

Behind the bar counter in the main white room, the back wall boasts curvy backlit elements from the airline's advertising. But the

BEST
Communist conversion

CHARLOTTE COCKTAIL

This cocktail contains a forgotten 'old German lady', namely egg liqueur, and is dedicated to another old German lady, the mother of CSA-Bar proprietor René Flatau. Egg liqueur was a favourite tipple of the women of René's mother's generation.

SERVES 1

dash of brown sugar
40 ml/1½ fl oz egg liqueur
 such as Advocaat
30 ml/1 fl oz golden rum
10 ml/⅓ fl oz Red Orange
 curaçao
60 ml/2 fl oz fresh orange juice

Chill a champagne flute or coupette and rim it with the brown sugar by pressing it into a wet paper towel and then dipping it into a saucer of sugar. Shake the egg liqueur, golden rum, curaçao and orange juice over ice cubes, and double-strain the mixture into the glass.

'I wanted to create a timeless style and place. Converting the former CSA airline office into a cocktail bar seemed to be a perfect way of fusing past, present and future.'

Proprietor, René Flatau

...ar itself is sleek and modern. The tables in the private 'salons' ...t each end of the bar have built-in spinning ashtrays from the ...960s, but the couches on which guests sit are the very epitome ...f contemporary elegance. It's all a far cry from the kitschy *Ostalgie* (nostalgia for the former East) one might expect in ...his neighbourhood.

 Soft spotlights cast a flattering glow, while tall plate-glass windows ...verlook the bustling wide street. When it snows – as it does in Berlin ...n the winter – the scene outside resembles a romantic postcard.

 Back inside, there's a long cocktail list to warm you, while jazz and ...ounge music mellow the mood. Despite the chic surroundings, the ...tmosphere is very congenial and no critic seems to visit CSA without ...emarking on the friendly service. Let the staff know your general ...aste in drinks and they'll produce something just right for you.

CSA-BAR
Karl-Marx-Allee 96,
Friedrichshain
10243 Berlin
Germany
+49 30 290 44 741
www.csa-bar.de

Open daily
8.00 p.m. until the last customer leaves

THE MORNING AFTER

Do you have an urgent need to get back to the land of the living?
If you are one of those people who swear by hair of the dog, these
tried and trusted recipes will cast out a furry tongue and banish
a barking headache. If you are not, you may find it's a question
of kill or cure…

PRAIRIE OYSTER ◄

This is, without doubt, the ultimate hangover cure.
It should be gulped down in one go.

SERVES 1
1 measure brandy
1 tsp Worcestershire sauce
2 dashes of Tabasco sauce
salt
freshly ground pepper
1 egg

*Shake the brandy, Worcestershire sauce and Tabasco
sauce over ice cubes until well frosted. Add salt and
freshly ground pepper to taste, and strain into a chilled
old-fashioned glass or lowball glass. Crack the egg into
the glass, taking special care not to break the yolk.*

In the film *Cabaret*, Sally Bowles, played by Liza
Minnelli, makes a Prairie Oyster for her flat-mate Brian
Roberts, played by Michael York, although his turns out
to have a weird peppermint taste as she's accidentally
made it in her toothpaste glass.

It is vital not to scramble the egg yolk and you're
supposed to gulp it down in one go, which may be for
the best given that some people find a Prairie Oyster
somewhat unappealing.

Celery salt and cayenne pepper are additions you
can make to a Prairie Oyster. Another twist is the
Bloody Prairie Oyster – essentially a Bloody Mary
with a raw egg yolk dropped into it.

APPLE RUM RICKEY

SERVES 1
1 measure apple brandy
½ measure white rum
½ measure lime juice
cracked ice
sparkling water
lime slice

Pour the apple brandy, white rum and lime juice over ice cubes and shake vigorously until well frosted. Half fill a chilled highball glass with cracked ice and strain the cocktail over it. Top up with sparkling water and dress with a slice of lime.

BLOODHOUND ▸

This is a rather light, delicate drink – see if you can sniff out the ingredients.

SERVES 1
2 measures gin
1 measure sweet vermouth
1 measure dry vermouth
3 strawberries
crushed ice

Whizz the gin, sweet vermouth, dry vermouth and strawberries in a small blender with a little crushed ice until smooth. Strain into a chilled cocktail glass.

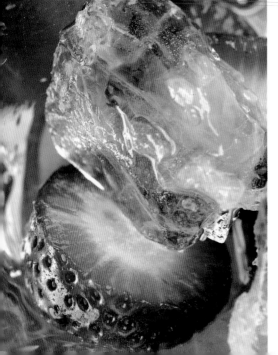

BULLSHOT

This is not unlike drinking chilled consommé, but with a kick. It is best really cold.

SERVES 1
1 measure vodka
2 measures beef consommé or good stock
dash of fresh lemon juice
2 dashes of Worcestershire sauce
cracked ice
celery salt
lemon peel

Pour the vodka, beef consommé, lemon juice and Worcestershire sauce over ice cubes and shake vigorously until well frosted. Put the cracked ice in a cocktail glass and strain the cocktail over it. Sprinkle with celery salt and dress with a strip of lemon peel.

PERFECT LOVE

SERVES 1
1 measure vodka
½ measure Parfait Amour
½ measure maraschino
scoop of crushed ice

Shake together the vodka, Parfait Amour and maraschino over ice cubes until frosted. Put some crushed ice into a chilled cocktail glass and strain the cocktail over it.

CUPID

SERVES 1
2 measures dry sherry
1 tsp sugar syrup
1 egg
dash of Tabasco sauce

Pour the dry sherry, sugar syrup, egg and dash of Tabasco sauce over ice cubes and shake vigorously until well frosted. Strain into a chilled cocktail glass.

The name of this cocktail is a literal translation of the name of one of its ingredients: Parfait Amour is an unusual purple liqueur flavoured with rose petals, almonds and vanilla.

BROWN COW

If you're not worth a damn 'til you've had your
morning coffee, this is a rather good way of taking it.

SERVES 1
cracked ice
1 measure Kahlúa
3 measures milk, chilled

*Pour the Kahlúa and chilled milk over cracked ice and
shake vigorously until well frosted. Half fill a chilled lowball
glass with cracked ice and strain the cocktail over it.*

FERDINAND THE BULL

There isn't any alcohol in this, but it may make you
feel bullish nonetheless.

SERVES 1
4 measures tomato juice
4 measures beef stock, chilled
1 measure lime juice
dash of Worcestershire sauce
dash of Tabasco sauce
cracked ice
salt and freshly ground black pepper
lime wedge

*Shake all the liquids over ice cubes until well frosted. Half
fill a chilled highball glass with cracked ice and strain
the cocktail over it. Season to taste with salt and freshly
ground black pepper, and decorate with a lime wedge.*

WHITE COSMOPOLITAN

Nothing like its pink cousin the Cosmopolitan (page
149), this is far more fruity and, instead of vodka,
is based on a punchy lemon-flavoured liqueur.

SERVES 1
1½ measures Limoncello
½ measure Cointreau
1 measure white cranberry and grape juice
dash of orange bitters
a few red cranberries

*Shake together the Limoncello, Cointreau and white
cranberry and grape juice over ice cubes until well
frosted. Strain into a chilled cocktail glass, add a dash
of orange bitters and dress with cranberries.*

MINT SUNRISE ‹

SERVES 1
cracked ice
1½ measures Scotch whisky
½ measure brandy
½ measure white curaçao
fresh mint sprig

Pour the Scotch whisky, brandy and white curaçao over cracked ice in a chilled highball or lowball glass and stir gently. Decorate with a sprig of fresh mint.

Pick-me-ups like the Widow's Wish have traditionally included a raw egg as a way of delivering easily digested protein and providing the extra energy needed the day after the night before.

OCEAN BREEZE

This is a breeze to make and as colourful as the whipped-up ocean on an early morning – just don't dilute too much.

SERVES 1
1 measure white rum
1 measure amaretto
½ measure blue curaçao
½ measure pineapple juice
soda water

Shake together the white rum, amaretto, blue curaçao and pineapple juice over ice cubes. Pour into a highball glass and top up with soda water to taste.

WIDOW'S WISH

SERVES 1
2 measures Benedictine
1 egg
single cream

Pour the Benedictine and the egg over ice cubes and shake vigorously until well frosted. Strain into a chilled lowball glass and top up with single cream.

SUFFERING FOOL

SERVES 1
1 tbsp Angostura bitters
cracked ice
2 measures gin
1½ measures brandy
½ measure lime juice
1 tsp sugar syrup
ginger beer
cucumber slice
lime slice
fresh mint sprig

*Pour the Angostura bitters into a chilled highball glass
and swirl around. Discard the excess. Half fill the glass with
cracked ice. Pour the gin, brandy, lime juice and sugar
syrup over the ice and stir well. Top up with ginger beer
and stir gently. Dress with cucumber, lime and mint.*

NINETEEN PICK-ME-UP ▸

SERVES 1
2 measures Pernod
1 measure gin
¼ tsp sugar syrup
dash of Angostura bitters
cracked ice
sparkling water

*Pour the Pernod, gin, sugar syrup and Angostura bitters
over ice cubes and shake vigorously until well frosted.
Half fill a highball glass with cracked ice and strain the
cocktail over it. Top up with sparkling water.*

MOONLIGHT

SERVES 1
2 measures apple brandy
2 measures lemon juice
½ tsp sugar syrup
cracked ice

*Pour the apple brandy, lemon juice and sugar syrup over
ice cubes and shake vigorously until well frosted. Half fill
a chilled lowball glass with cracked ice and strain the
cocktail over it.*

If you're already suffering, the Nineteen Pick-Me-Up could be a cure, but on the other hand it could be the cause of suffering still to come – you'll have to make up your own mind.

HOT AND DIRTY MARTINI ▲

A Martini, yes, but one that will really put fire in your belly for the day ahead.

SERVES 1
3 measures chilli vodka
½ measure dry vermouth
1 tsp olive brine
stuffed olive

Shake the chilli vodka, dry vermouth and olive brine over ice cubes until well frosted. Strain into a chilled martini or cocktail glass and dress with a stuffed olive.

FROZEN PINEAPPLE DAIQUIRI ▲

SERVES 1
crushed ice
2 measures white rum
1 measure lime juice
½ tsp pineapple syrup
60 g/2 oz fresh pineapple, finely chopped
pineapple wedges

Whizz the crushed ice in a blender with the white rum, lime juice, pineapple syrup and fresh pineapple until slushy. Pour into a chilled cocktail glass and dress with wedges of pineapple.

SALTY DOG

SERVES 1

1 tbsp granulated sugar
1 tbsp coarse salt
lime wedge
6–8 ice cubes, cracked
2 measures vodka
grapefruit juice

Mix the sugar and salt in a saucer. Rub the rim of a chilled highball glass with a lime wedge, then dip it into the sugar and salt mixture to frost. Fill the glass with cracked ice and pour the vodka over it. Top up with grapefruit juice and stir to mix.

PLANTER'S PUNCH REFRESHER

SERVES 1

1 measure rum
1 measure lime juice
1–2 tsp grenadine
dash of Angostura bitters
cracked ice
soda water or sparkling mineral water

Vigorously shake the rum, lime juice, grenadine and Angostura bitters over ice cubes until well frosted. Half fill a chilled highball glass with cracked ice, strain the cocktail over it and top up with soda water.

When this cocktail first appeared, gin-based mixes were by far the most popular, but nowadays a Salty Dog is more frequently made with vodka. Choose whichever you prefer, but the cocktails will have different flavours.

GINGER BEER ◀

Yes, it's ginger beer, but not as you normally know it.

SERVES 1
250 ml/8 fl oz bitter
2 measures ginger brandy

Pour the bitter into a chilled beer glass or tankard and then add the ginger brandy.

WOO-WOO

SERVES 1
cracked ice
2 measures vodka
2 measures peach schnapps
4 measures cranberry juice

Half fill a chilled highball glass with cracked ice. Pour the vodka, peach schnapps and cranberry juice over the ice, and stir well to mix.

MOONSHOT ▲

SERVES 1
cracked ice
dash of Tabasco sauce
2 measures gin
3 measures clam juice
celery stick

Put some cracked ice into a mixing glass. Dash the Tabasco sauce over the ice and pour in the gin and clam juice. Stir well to mix, then strain into a chilled highball or lowball glass. Dress with a stick of celery.

FUZZY NAVEL

SERVES 1
cracked ice
2 measures vodka
1 measure peach schnapps
250 ml/8 fl oz orange juice
physalis

Pour the vodka, peach schnapps and orange juice over cracked ice and shake vigorously until well frosted. Strain into a chilled cocktail glass and dress with a physalis.

The Fuzzy Navel is another one of those cocktails with a name that plays on the ingredients – fuzzy to remind you that it contains peach schnapps and navel because it is mixed with orange juice.

BRANDY COBBLER ▲

SERVES 1
1 tsp caster sugar
3 measures sparkling water
cracked ice
2 measures brandy
lemon slice
cocktail cherry

Put the caster sugar into a small chilled lowball glass and add the sparkling water. Stir until the sugar has dissolved, then fill the glass with cracked ice. Pour in the brandy and stir well. Dress with a slice of lemon and a cocktail cherry.

RUM COBBLER ▸

SERVES 1
1 tsp caster sugar
2 measures sparkling water
cracked ice
2 measures white rum
lime slice
orange slice

Put the caster sugar into a chilled wine glass. Add the sparkling water and stir until the sugar has dissolved. Fill the glass with cracked ice and pour in the white rum. Stir well and dress with slices of lime and orange.

DOG'S NOSE ◂

SERVES 1
250 ml/8 fl oz pale ale
1 measure gin

Pour the pale ale into a chilled beer glass or tankard and then add the gin.

RIKKI-TIKKI-TAVI ▸

SERVES 1
1 sugar cube
dash of Angostura bitters
1 tsp brandy
1 tsp white curaçao
champagne, chilled

Put the sugar cube into a chilled flute and dash the Angostura bitters over it until it is red but still intact. Pour in the brandy and white curaçao, and top up with chilled champagne.

YORSH ▴

SERVES 1
250 ml/8 fl oz pale ale
2 measures vodka

Pour the pale ale into a chilled beer glass or tankard and then add the vodka.

Rikki-Tikki-Tavi is a mongoose in a short story of the same name by Rudyard Kipling. Quite what the cocktail has to do with a mongoose is anybody's guess, but the drink will certainly give you a lift.

PACIFIC SUNRISE ◂

SERVES 1

1 measure white tequila

1 measure blue curaçao

1 measure lime juice

dash of bitters

Pour the white tequila, blue curaçao, lime juice and dash of bitters over ice cubes and shake vigorously until well frosted. Strain into a chilled cocktail glass.

ABSINTHE FRIEND

The original absinthe was a popular cocktail ingredient and digestif, but any pastis, such as Pernod and Ricard, will do just as well instead.

SERVES 1

1 measure gin

1 measure absinthe or Pernod

dash of Angostura bitters

dash of sugar syrup

Pour the gin, absinthe, Angostura bitters and sugar syrup over ice cubes and shake vigorously until well frosted. Strain into a chilled lowball glass.

CHAMPAGNE PICK-ME-UP ▲

A glass of this delicious cocktail and you'll be bubbling over with energy.

SERVES 1

2 measures brandy

1 measure orange juice

1 measure lemon juice

dash of grenadine

champagne, chilled

Pour the brandy, orange juice, lemon juice and a dash of grenadine over ice cubes and shake vigorously until well frosted. Strain the mixture into a wine glass or flute and then top up with chilled champagne.

WALLIS SIMPSON ▸

SERVES 1
1 measure Southern Comfort
1 tsp caster sugar
dash of Angostura bitters
champagne, chilled
orange slice

Pour the Southern Comfort into a chilled champagne flute, add the caster sugar and stir well until dissolved. Add the dash of Angostura bitters and top up with chilled champagne. Dress with a slice of orange.

STARS AND SWIRLS

You will need a steady hand for this one – preferably two pairs of steady hands.

SERVES 1
1 measure Malibu
large ice cube
½ measure strawberry or raspberry liqueur
1 tsp blue curaçao

Chill a small shot glass really well. Pour in the Malibu and add the large ice cube. Carefully pour in the other two liqueurs – the red strawberry and the blue curaçao – simultaneously, from opposite sides of the glass. Do this very slowly, so that they slip down the sides of the glass and swirl around.

FROZEN PEACH DAIQUIRI ▸

SERVES 1
crushed ice
2 measures white rum
1 measure lime juice
1 tsp sugar syrup
half a peach, peeled, stoned and chopped
peach slice

Whizz the crushed ice in a blender with the white rum, lime juice, sugar syrup and chopped peach until slushy. Pour into a chilled cocktail glass and dress with a slice of peach.

BLINDING SUNRISE ‹

SERVES 1
1 measure white tequila
1 measure vodka
3 measures orange juice
1 tsp triple sec
cracked ice
1 measure grenadine

Pour the white tequila, vodka, orange juice and triple sec over ice cubes and shake vigorously until well frosted. Half fill a highball glass with cracked ice and strain the cocktail over. Slowly pour in the grenadine.

CORPSE REVIVER

After a heavy night, as the name suggests, this cocktail will keep you going and even put you in the mood for another party.

SERVES 1
cracked ice
2 measures brandy
1 measure apple brandy
1 measure sweet vermouth

Pour the brandy, apple brandy and vermouth into a mixing glass over cracked ice. Stir gently to mix and strain into a chilled cocktail glass.

KAMIKAZE

Drinking this cocktail may be an act of extreme recklessness, but it is so delicious you won't be able to put it down.

SERVES 1
1 measure vodka
1 measure triple sec
½ measure fresh lime juice
½ measure fresh lemon juice
dry white wine, chilled
lime slice
cucumber slice

Shake together vodka, triple sec, lime juice and lemon juice over ice cubes until well frosted. Strain into a chilled highball glass and top up with chilled white wine. Dress with slices of lime and cucumber.

BREAKFAST

It's got the egg, but no bacon – if you've been partying all night and it's now time for breakfast, see if you've got the stomach for this.

SERVES 1
cracked ice
2 measures gin
1 measure grenadine
1 egg yolk

Pour the gin and grenadine over cracked ice in a shaker and add the egg yolk. Shake vigorously until well frosted and strain into a chilled lowball glass.

PUROBEACH OASIS DEL MAR

PALMA DE MALLORCA

Yoga and massages in the morning, Mojitos and DJs in the evening – that's the beguiling conceptual mix that's made PuroBeach in Mallorca the favourite open-air bar of discerning critics. Luxury guides such as *Mr and Mrs Smith*, *Condé Nast Traveller* and PuroBeach's well-heeled European customers all agree this man-made peninsula jutting into the Bay of Palma is the coolest beach bar in the Balearics.

The gleaming white complex consists of a revamped Art Deco pavilion and a terraced pool backing right on to the sea. On the pavilion's ground level, there's a restaurant and bar; below them there is a spa with treatment rooms.

BEST
beach bar

ULTRA VIOLET

This extremely popular long drink fits perfectly with the hot summer nights at Puro.

SERVES 1

80 ml/2¾ fl oz Absolut Kurant vodka

40 ml/1½ fl oz blue curaçao

2 tsp strawberry syrup

2 tsp grenadine

soda water

star fruit slices

Shake together the vodka, blue curaçao, strawberry syrup and grenadine. Half fill a highball glass with ice cubes then pour over the liquid. Top up with soda water and garnish with slices of star fruit.

❖

'PuroBeach offers wellbeing in a club environment, so our guests can combine a morning yoga session with the chance to enjoy a chilled Puro Rosé Daiquiri in the evening.'

Manager, Peter Estebe

Before sunset, hedonists catch a few rays on the terrace's white sun-loungers. Other guests lounge on the restaurant's low white sofas and puff chairs, taking advantage of its wide open porch to enjoy the wonderful views, meanwhile dining on seafood and excellent fusion cuisine.

The interior design has been described as Miami meets Marrakesh and that is certainly true in the bar. Here a large Moroccan shell lamp spans the ceiling and the lampshades are hung with hippy-chic shells.

And it's to the bar – and the terrace – that attention turns for the daily 'sunset ceremony'. The DJ switches from mellow eclectic and chilled beats to deep house and stylish tracks. Guests switch from smoothies to cocktails. During the beach bar's full-moon parties, celebrity DJs might spin the tunes.

PUROBEACH OASIS DEL MAR
Pagel 1
Cala Estancia
Palma de Mallorca
+34 971 744 744
www.purobeach.com

Open daily
March to October 11.00 a.m.
  to 2.00 a.m.
November to February
Monday to Thursday 11.00 a.m.
  to 7.00 p.m.
Friday to Sunday 11.00 a.m. to 1.00 a.m.

COCKTAIL INDEX

Cocktail index

GENERAL INDEX